THE
SOUP
COOKBOOK

THE
SOUP
COOKBOOK

Recipes to warm the heart

First published in 2011
LOVE FOOD is an imprint of Parragon Books Ltd
Parragon
Queen Street House
4 Queen Street
Bath BA1 1HE, UK

ISBN: 978-1-4454-4327-0

Printed in China

Cover illustration by Georgina Luck, www.georginaluck.com
Introduction by Christine McFadden

This book uses imperial, metric, and US cup measurements. Follow the same units of measurement
throughout; do not mix imperial and metric. All spoon measurements are level: teaspoons are assumed
to be 5 ml, and tablespoons are assumed to be 15 ml. Unless otherwise stated, milk is assumed to
be whole, eggs and individual vegetables, such as potatoes, are medium, and pepper is freshly ground
black pepper.

The times given are an approximate guide only. Preparation times differ according to the techniques used
by different people and the cooking times may also vary from those given as a result of the type of oven
used. Optional ingredients, variations, or serving suggestions have not been included in the calculations.

Recipes using raw or very lightly cooked eggs should be avoided by infants, the elderly, pregnant women,
convalescents, and anyone with a chronic condition. Pregnant and breast-feeding women are advised
to avoid eating peanuts and peanut products. People with nut allergies should be aware that some of
the prepared ingredients used in the recipes in this book may contain nuts. Always check the package
before use.

Contents

Introduction

Taking a cook's look around the world, there is hardly a country that doesn't have its favorite soup—from North American chowders and Russian borscht to Spanish gazpacho and Scotch broth, and many more. This popularity is hardly surprising. Soups are comforting, appetizing, nutritious, and as easy on the pocket as on the waistline. They put to good use morsels of meat or fish, leftover rice and pasta, and vegetables that are slightly past their best. They simmer happily on the stove, leaving you free to relax or get on with other things. The ultimate in convenience, soups can be prepared in advance, then chilled or frozen, ready to reheat when needed. Soups are wonderfully adaptable—warming in winter and refreshing in summer, a well-made soup gives you a feeling of well-being, is satisfying but also easy to digest, and is suitable for a solitary supper or feeding a crowd.

Essential Ingredients for Soup Making

PANTRY INGREDIENTS

An impressive range of soups can be made from pantry ingredients. If you enjoy making soup and want to do so regularly, it's worth stocking up on the basics. Pantry items usually have a long shelf-life, but make sure you check the expiration dates regularly and discard any that are out of date.

Stock

Good-quality stock is the foundation of all good soups. Homemade stock has the best flavor, but store-bought stock is a useful fallback. Jellied or concentrated liquid stock is generally a good choice. Bouillon cubes vary in quality and tend to be too salty.

Oils

Flavorless vegetable oils, such as sunflower, grapeseed, or canola oil, are used for the preliminary softening of vegetables. Oils with a strong flavor, such as extra virgin olive oil or toasted sesame oil, are best reserved for a final drizzle before serving the soup. Store oils in a dark cupboard away from heat.

Pasta and noodles

Thin dried pasta and small shapes are essential for minestrone and other hearty mixed soups. Asian noodles add bulk and texture to clear soups. Cook them before adding to soup.

Grains

Rice, pearl barley, and spelt are satisfying additions to all kinds of soups. Naturally bland, they team well with robustly flavored vegetables and potent aromatics.

Dried beans

Classified as legumes, dried beans include lentils, split peas, and chickpeas. With their soft creamy texture and earthy flavors, they make some of the best-tasting soups. With the exception of lentils, dried beans need lengthy soaking and cooking before adding to soup. Canned dried beans and lentils are a convenient alternative because they do not need any precooking or soaking.

Salt

Salt is a must for soups—even a small amount will improve the flavor. Use free-flowing table salt for seasoning soup as it cooks. Sprinkle with a few sea salt flakes just before serving to provide crunchy texture and bursts of flavor.

Seasonings, sauces, and condiments

Sold in handy bottles and jars, these have a long shelf-life. A teaspoon of soy sauce will round out an Asian-style soup, as will a few drops of Thai fish sauce. Worcestershire sauce adds savory piquancy. Tabasco sauce has a powerful, fiery kick. Tomato or anchovy paste are also useful flavor boosters.

Spices

Spices add exciting flavors and fragrance to soups. The most useful are black pepper, chile flakes, cayenne pepper, paprika, cumin, and coriander seeds. Nutmeg and cinnamon also come in handy. Spices quickly lose their potency once ground, so buy them whole and grind as needed. Store in airtight containers in a cool, dark cupboard.

Dried herbs

Robust herbs, such as rosemary, oregano, sage, and thyme, keep their flavor when dried. Add to vegetables before adding stock so that they have time to release their flavors during the preliminary frying. Buy in small quantities and store in airtight containers in a dark cupboard away from heat.

Dried mushrooms

Morels, shiitake, and porcini have an exceptionally meaty flavor when dried. Soak in hot water for about 15 minutes before using. The drained soaking liquid can be added to stock.

Thickening agents

Flour-based thickeners bind liquids and solids in soups, holding the solids in suspension. To thicken 4 cups, sizzle 3 tablespoons of all-purpose flour with 2 tablespoons of butter, stirring until smooth, before gradually whisking in the liquid. Bring to a boil, then simmer for at least 5 minutes, stirring continuously.

Cornstarch, arrowroot, and potato flour are useful for thickening clear soups. They are quick to cook and produce a slightly glutinous texture. Mix to a thin paste with water before adding to hot liquid. Add toward the end of cooking, stirring well while thickening.

Rice flour is another option. It can be safely sprinkled directly into hot liquid, without forming unwanted lumps.

Vinegar

A few drops of wine vinegar or rice vinegar will sharpen the flavor of most soups. Balsamic vinegar is sweeter and syrupy, and is best used for drizzling on soup just before serving.

FRESH INGREDIENTS

A well-stocked refrigerator or pantry will not only provide the essentials for soup and stock, it will also help you create tasty garnishes and make the most of fresh seasonal produce.

Dairy products

Dairy products add richness and body to soups. They also provide valuable nutrients, such as protein and calcium.

Butter may be used for the preliminary softening of vegetables or swirled in at the end of cooking to round out the flavor.

Cheese is used mainly as a garnish. Hard cheeses, such as Parmesan and cheddar, are useful for grating. Melting cheeses, such as mozzarella and Gruyère, make tasty toppings for croûtes (see page 13). Crumbled feta adds a salty tang.

Cream and sour cream add rich flavors and silky texture. Do not add them to boiling soup, because they may curdle (see page 13 for advice on rescuing a curdled soup).

Plain yogurt cuts the flavor of rich soups or it can be used in its own right as a base for chilled soups. Avoid adding yogurt to boiling soup because it will curdle.

Fish and seafood

Fish and seafood have subtle flavors and a delicate texture. They need gentle cooking to prevent them from disintegrating or becoming tough.

Monkfish, halibut, and snapper fillets are the basis for mixed fish soups, such as bouillabaisse. Cut into large chunks and cook gently until opaque.

Salmon is good in light soups, either with young spring vegetables or thin noodles. Use chunks cut from meaty cutlets, or strips from the tail end, where there are fewer bones.

Shrimp, fresh or frozen, are indispensable for Asian-style clear soups or creamy laksas. You may prefer to devein shrimp before you use them—that is, to remove the black line (the intestinal tract) running along the back of each shrimp. Cook shrimp quickly until opaque. Do not overcook or they will become tough.

Clams are a traditional ingredient in creamy chowders. Scrub and rinse well before using.

Meat

Meat makes nourishing soups with deeply satisfying flavors. A little goes a long way and cheaper cuts become meltingly tender after leisurely simmering. Leftover cooked meat can also be used in soups.

Beef and lamb provide substantial flavors that stand up to potent spices, cabbage, and other strongly flavored vegetables. For slow-cooked soups, use cheaper cuts, such as beef flank or shoulder of lamb. Cut into bite-size chunks, removing any visible fat and gristle. Ground beef or lamb make flavorsome miniature meatballs to bulk out soups.

Pork has a distinctive slightly sweet flavor that is equally good with creamy soups or spicy, Asian-style soups. Use tenderloin or boneless chops, cut into thin strips or small cubes. Bacon is a useful ingredient for adding flavor to all kinds of soup.

Poultry

There are literally hundreds of poultry soups. They are universally popular and among the most comforting.

Chicken and turkey can be used more or less interchangeably. Cut the meat into thin strips or bite-size cubes, discarding the skin. The meat from thighs and drumsticks is more succulent than breast meat and has more flavor.

Duck produces flavorsome juices and is particularly good in Asian-style soups. Its characteristic sweetness goes well with spices, such as star anise and fennel. Cut the meat into thin strips or bite-size cubes, and remove the skin and fat.

Vegetables

The sheer versatility of vegetables makes them the basis for countless inspiring soups. They offer appetizing flavors, textures, and colors, and are a rich source of health-promoting vitamins and minerals.

Basics

Celery, carrots, and onions are essential for making stock. Together they create a complex flavor that is the foundation for all good soups.

Potatoes, parsnips, and celeriac provide body and earthy sweetness. Starchy potatoes can be mashed or pureed and used as a thickener.

Garlic, shallots, and leeks add mellow sweet flavors. They become meltingly soft as they cook down.

Leafy greens, such as spinach, cabbage, and Swiss chard, provide color, potent flavor, and vital vitamins. They are especially good added to meaty soups or those based on beans and pasta. Remove and discard tough stalks and slice the leaves into ribbons before adding to soup. Spinach and Swiss chard produce plenty of extra liquid, so you may need less stock.

Seasonal vegetables

Asparagus, young peas, zucchini, and corn make deliciously fresh-tasting summery soups. Use them within 24 hours of picking or buying, while the flavors are at their best.

Arugula and watercress make vibrant, peppery soups. Add potato or cream to give the soup body.

Tomatoes and bell peppers are at their best in mid-to-late summer. They are delicious in chilled gazpacho and other Mediterranean-style soups.

Pumpkins and butternut squash make colorful fall soups. Cut into wedges and roast them to boost the flavor, then blend to a rich velvety puree.

Jerusalem artichokes have a unique nutty flavor. Cook them in milk and stock for a fortifying winter soup.

Mushrooms lend a sweet, earthy taste to all kinds of soups. They are perfect for adding body and flavor to meat soups and are a great additional to Asian-style soups. To clean, wipe mushrooms with damp paper towels or brush gently—do not immerse in water.

Pureeing Soups

Some soups need to be pureed to make them smoother or more palatable. Exceptions are clear soups, such as chicken noodle soup, and chunky soups, such as minestrone. There are also semipureed soups in which only about half to two-thirds of the soup is pureed. The resulting liquid is then combined with the reserved solid ingredients, which give the soup an interesting texture as well as an indication of what went into it.

Your choice of utensil will depend on the amount to be pureed, how smooth you want the soup to be, and whether you prefer the speed of an electrically powered machine or are happy to do the job by hand.

Blender

For a really silky smooth soup, it's best to use a blender. The blades whirl at a higher speed than a food processor, producing a finer textured puree. The narrow pitcher keeps solid ingredients within reach of the blades, so you don't have to keep stopping and stirring. It's a good idea to hold down the lid with a folded cloth because the contents can rise up and overflow when the blades start to rotate, especially if the soup is still hot. To prevent mishaps, it's best not to fill the pitcher past the halfway point.

Food processor

The bowl of a food processor can cope with larger quantities than a blender. The pulse button makes it easy to control the texture, although the end result will not be as smooth as soup from a blender because the wider base means that less of the soup comes in contact with the blades.

Handheld blender

Handy for pureeing soup directly in the pan, handheld blenders have a short horizontal blade at the end of a rotating metal stick. As you move it around the pan, it breaks down solids, producing a reasonably smooth puree. The real bonus of using a handheld blender is that it is much easier to clean than other utensils—the blade end is usually detachable and simply needs to be rinsed under running water.

Food mill/moulis-légumes

One of the most useful nonelectric gadgets, the food mill resembles a colander with folding feet that clamp over a bowl to hold it steady. It is fitted with a spring-mounted handle that clips over a perforated metal disk. As you rotate the handle, the food is pushed through the disk and the resulting puree drops into the bowl below.

Conical strainer/chinois

Also called a "bouillon strainer," this deep cone-shape strainer is ideal for producing very smooth purees by hand. The ultrafine mesh clears stocks of every trace of sediment and strains softened vegetables to a velvety puree. It comes with a tapered wooden pestle that fits into the bottom of the cone, and presses the last drop of liquid from solid ingredients.

Garnishes & Serving Suggestions

GARNISHES

Attractive garnishes sharpen the appetite and reflect the character of the soup. When choosing garnishes, aim for contrasting color and texture, and a flavor that complements the soup.

Herbs

A sprinkling of fresh green herbs will bring any soup to life. Choose tender-leaved varieties, chop them coarsely, and add at the last minute.

Spices

Zesty spices, such as black peppercorns, cumin, or coriander seeds, add potent flavor to vegetable or bean-based soups. Grind them freshly and add just before serving. Add a pinch of crushed chile flakes or paprika for vibrant color.

Pesto and tapenade (black olive paste)

A slick of pesto will add sharpness and brilliant color to pasta or bean soups. Inky tapenade goes particularly well with tomato or red bell pepper soups.

Oils

Trickled over soup just before serving, extra virgin olive oil adds richness, color, and smoothness. Toasted sesame oil is good with Asian-style soups.

Nuts and seeds

Chopped toasted nuts add flavor and crunch to pureed vegetable soups. Pumpkin, sunflower, and sesame seeds also add texture and color.

Bacon

Snippets of crisp-fried bacon add flavor, color, and texture to pale pureed soups.

Vegetables

Sizzled wisps of carrot, parsnip, or leek make a stunning garnish to pureed or cream soups. Chopped scallion tops or seeded diced tomato add vibrant color.

Cream and yogurt

A swirl of cream or yogurt adds richness to mild-flavored soups and tames the heat of spicy soups. To prevent curdling, never add to boiling soup but add it off the heat, just before serving. Heavy cream has a high fat content and is less likely to curdle than lower-fat varieties, such as sour cream or light cream. Thick Greek yogurt is less likely to curdle than ordinary yogurt.

Aioli (see page 168)

A rich garlicky mayonnaise, delicious with Mediterranean fish or vegetable soups.

Rouille (see page 167)

A powerful, red garlicky sauce from Provence in France, traditionally served with bouillabaisse and other fish soups. Spread it on croûtes or swirl directly into the soup.

SERVING SUGGESTIONS

Soup can sometimes leave you feeling temporarily full but not necessarily satisfied. A tasty accompaniment will transform this light meal into something more hearty and substantial.

Breads

Bread is the perfect partner to a bowl of steaming soup. It adds bulk and also lets you mop up every last drop from the bowl. Nowadays, there is a wonderful choice available from bakeries and grocery stores, ranging from traditional sliced loaves to specialty breads from all over the world. If you want to try your hand at making your own breads, you will find plenty of tasty recipes in Chapter 6 of this book (see pages 202–221).

Ciabatta is an Italian slipper-shaped bread with an open texture and crisp crust. Good with minestrone or tomato-based soups.

Flatbreads are yeast-free breads that include chewy naan, chapattis, pitas, tortillas, and wraps. Use them to wipe out the soup bowl or break into small pieces and stir into the soup for added bulk.

Focaccia is a salty Italian flattened bread with a dimpled surface, sometimes topped with rosemary or onion. Excellent for mopping up Italian soups.

Garlic bread is made from Italian or French bread that has been spread with garlic butter and heated in the oven. Good with Mediterranean-style soups.

Sourdough is a traditional slow-fermented loaf with a slightly tangy flavor. Goes well with most soups.

Croutons (see page 205)

Cubes of day-old bread, fried until golden and crisp. Good for adding contrasting crunch to smooth, creamy soups.

Croûtes

Thick slices of oven-dried French bread, served plain or garnished with various toppings. Useful for padding out thinnish soups.

To make plain croûtes, slice a thin, day-old baguette and arrange on a baking sheet. Bake in a preheated oven at 350°F/180°C, turning once, for about 5 minutes, until golden and crisp.

To make cheese croûtes, bake the baguette slices for 1–2 minutes, until just crisp. Brush one side with melted butter and top with grated cheese or a slice of goat cheese. Return to the oven and bake until the cheese has melted.

TROUBLESHOOTING

When you're new to making soup, or even if you've been doing it a while, there are a few common problems that occasionally crop up.

• The soup is too thick: Dilute with extra stock or other liquid, depending on the type of soup. Reheat thoroughly and adjust the seasoning as necessary.

• The soup is too thin: Try adding cooked mashed potato or another starchy vegetable. Alternatively, thicken with breadcrumbs, finely ground nuts, or all-purpose flour (see pages 8–9). Make sure the flour is thoroughly cooked either before or after it goes in the soup.

• Pureed soup is lumpy: Process again briefly in a blender. Be careful not to overprocess because potatoes can become gluey. Alternatively, push the puree through a strainer.

• The soup is too salty: Add 2 peeled potatoes, simmer for 15 minutes, then remove them. The potatoes will absorb some of the salt. Alternatively, try adding extra liquid, such as milk, cream, or low-sodium stock. This will increase the proportion of liquid to salt and reduce the salty taste.

• The soup is too bland: Add a few drops of vinegar or lemon juice to brighten the flavor.

• Cream or yogurt has curdled: The soup was too hot when the cream was added. You may be able to rescue it by combining 1 tablespoon of cornstarch with 1½ tablespoons of water for every 2 cups of soup. Mix to a smooth paste, stir in a cupful of soup, then whisk the mixture into the remaining soup. Heat gently for 5 minutes, stirring, to cook the cornstarch. Process in batches in a blender, then push through a fine strainer before reheating gently. The flavor will be bland, so you may need to add more salt.

Making Fresh Stock

Homemade stock will lift an otherwise ordinary soup, giving it a rich, satisfying flavor. The basic method is always the same: the ingredients are simmered very gently in water until all the flavor is extracted. The exact time depends on the type of stock; vegetable stock takes about 30 minutes, while brown stock needs 2–3 hours.

Tips

• Always start off with cold water. If you try to speed up the process with hot water, you will end up with murky stock.
• Add enough cold water to cover the ingredients by no more than 2 inches/5 cm.
• Bring stock to a boil slowly. This lets foam collect on the surface, where it can be easily skimmed off.
• Never let stock boil for more than a few minutes, or you will end up with muddy liquid.
• Unless specified in the stock recipe, do not add salt. The flavor intensifies as the stock reduces and may become overpowering. Add it when you make the soup.
• Remove the layer of fat before using stock. It will solidify once chilled and be easy to lift off.

Storing stock

• Do not let stock cool in the stockpot. It must be cooled quickly and stored in the refrigerator without delay.
• Decant into smaller containers to speed up cooling.
• Once completely cold, store in sealed plastic containers in the refrigerator for 4–5 days, or in the freezer for 4–6 months.

ESSENTIAL EQUIPMENT

Stockpot
The tall, narrow shape keeps evaporation to a minimum, which in turn means that the contents remain submerged in liquid. The most useful size is 10 quarts—remember it can always double up as a pasta pot.

Perforated skimmer
The extra-wide flat bowl scoops up foam that rises to the surface as the stock heats.

Colander
Use for straining bones and vegetables. Make sure it has a sturdy lip or ear-shaped handles for resting on a saucepan or bowl.

Cheesecloth
Use for a second straining to filter out fat and sediment. Arrange a double thickness of damp cheesecloth in a strainer set over a bowl, then pour in previously strained stock.

Brown Stock
Makes about 5 cups

2 lb/900 g meat bones, raw or cooked
1 large onion
1 large carrot
2 celery stalks
1 bouquet garni*
7 cups water

1 Preheat the oven to 400°F/200°C. Place the bones in a roasting pan and cook in the preheated oven for 20 minutes, or until browned. Remove from the oven and let cool.
2 Meanwhile, cut the onion, carrots, and celery into large dice and set aside.
3 Chop the bones into small pieces and place in a large saucepan with the vegetables and bouquet garni. Pour in the water and slowly bring to a boil, skimming off any foam that rises to the surface. Reduce the heat, cover, and simmer for 2 hours.
4 Strain the stock into a bowl and let cool. Cover and store in the refrigerator. When cold, remove and discard the layer of fat from the surface.

* For a fresh bouquet garni, place 1 piece of celery, 1–2 small pieces of celery stalk with leaves, 2–3 cloves, 1 bay leaf, a few black peppercorns, 2–3 fresh parsley sprigs, and 1 fresh thyme sprig in the center of a small piece of cheesecloth, then tie up with a long length of kitchen string, which can then be tied to the pan handle for easy removal.

Chicken Stock
Makes about 10 cups

1 chicken, weighing about 2 lb 4 oz/1 kg
3 carrots
5 shallots
1 onion
1 leek
2 celery stalks
1 garlic bulb
17 cups water
1 fresh rosemary sprig
1 fresh thyme sprig
2 bay leaves
1 tsp white peppercorns
5 cloves
3 fresh parsley sprigs

1 Cut the chicken into large pieces. Cut the carrots, shallots, onion, leek, and celery into large chunks. Cut the garlic bulb in half horizontally.
2 Pour the water into a large saucepan and add the chicken. Slowly bring to a boil, skimming off any foam that rises to the surface. Add the vegetables, garlic, rosemary, thyme, bay leaves, peppercorns, and cloves, and simmer, occasionally skimming off the foam from the surface, for about 45 minutes.
3 Just before the stock is cooked, add the parsley and remove from the heat.
4 Remove the chicken pieces and set aside for later use. Strain the stock into a bowl and let cool. Cover and store in the refrigerator. When cold, remove and discard the layer of fat from the surface.

Vegetable Stock
Makes about 9 cups

½ fennel bulb
1 leek
3 carrots
2 celery stalks
2 onions
1 tomato
1 garlic bulb
10 cups water
1 fresh rosemary sprig
1 bay leaf
1 tsp white peppercorns
½ tsp fennel seeds

1 Remove any brown spots from the fennel and cut into large dice.
2 Cut the leek, carrots, celery, and onions into large dice. Cut the tomato and garlic bulb in half horizontally.
3 Pour the water into a large saucepan and add all the vegetables. Add the garlic, rosemary, bay leaf, peppercorns, and fennel seeds, slowly bring to a boil and simmer for about 20 minutes.
4 Strain the stock into a bowl and let cool. Cover and store in the refrigerator.

Fish Stock
Makes about 10 cups

2 lb 4 oz/1 kg white fish heads, bones, and trimmings, rinsed
1 onion
3 shallots
½ fennel bulb
3 celery stalks
1 garlic bulb
3 tbsp vegetable oil
10 white peppercorns
½ tsp fennel seeds
1 tbsp sea salt
2 bay leaves
generous 1 cup white wine
3 tbsp dry vermouth
6⅓ cups water
2 lemon slices
1 fresh basil sprig
1 fresh thyme sprig

1 Cut out and discard the gills from any fish heads, then soak the fish heads, bones, and trimmings for 30 minutes.
2 Cut the onion, shallots, fennel, and celery into medium dice. Cut the garlic bulb in half horizontally.
3 Heat the oil in a large saucepan, add the vegetables and cook for 5 minutes, until softened but not browned. Add the garlic, peppercorns, fennel seeds, sea salt, and bay leaves.
4 Drain the fish well, then add to the pan and sweat briefly. Add the wine, vermouth, and water and slowly bring to a simmer, skimming off any foam that rises to the surface.
5 Simmer gently, occasionally skimming off the foam from the surface, for about 15 minutes. Add the lemon slices, basil, and thyme and simmer for an additional 5 minutes.
6 Strain the stock into a bowl and let cool. Cover and store in the refrigerator.

Chapter 1
Summer Vegetable Soups

Creamy Tomato
& Basil Soup

Serves 6

ingredients

- 2 tbsp butter
- 1 tbsp olive oil
- 1 onion, finely chopped
- 1 garlic clove, chopped
- 2 lb/900 g plum tomatoes, chopped
- 2¾ cups vegetable stock
- ½ cup dry white wine
- 2 tbsp sun-dried tomato paste
- 2 tbsp torn fresh basil leaves, plus extra whole leaves to garnish
- ⅔ cup heavy cream
- salt and pepper

1 Melt the butter with the oil in a large, heavy-bottom pan. Add the onion and cook, stirring occasionally, for 5 minutes, or until softened. Add the garlic, tomatoes, stock, wine, and tomato paste, stir well, and season to taste with salt and pepper. Partially cover the pan and simmer, stirring occasionally, for 20–25 minutes, or until the mixture is soft and pulpy.

2 Remove the saucepan from the heat and let cool slightly. Transfer to a food processor or blender, in batches if necessary, add the torn basil, and process to a puree. Push the mixture through a strainer into the rinsed-out pan.

3 Stir the cream into the soup and reheat gently, but do not let it boil. Ladle the soup into warmed bowls, garnish with the whole basil leaves, and serve immediately.

Minestrone

Serves 6

ingredients

- 2 tbsp olive oil
- 1 Bermuda onion, chopped
- 2 garlic cloves, finely chopped
- 2 celery stalks, chopped
- 4 slices bacon, diced
- ½ small white cabbage, cored and shredded
- ⅔ cup red wine
- 7½ cups vegetable stock
- ⅓ cup dried cannellini beans, soaked overnight, and drained
- 4 plum tomatoes, peeled, seeded, and chopped
- 2 tbsp tomato paste
- 2 tsp sugar
- 2 carrots, diced
- ½ cup fresh shelled peas
- 2 cups 1-inch/2.5-cm green bean pieces
- 2oz/55g dried ziti pasta
- 2 tbsp chopped fresh mixed herbs
- salt and pepper
- freshly grated Parmesan cheese, to serve

1 Heat the oil in a large pan. Add the onion, garlic, celery, and bacon, and cook over low heat, stirring occasionally, for 5–7 minutes, until the onion has softened and the bacon is crisp. Stir in the cabbage and cook, stirring frequently, for another 5 minutes.

2 Increase the heat to medium, pour in the wine, and cook for about 2 minutes, until the alcohol has evaporated, then pour in the vegetable stock. Add the cannellini beans and bring to a boil, then reduce the heat, cover, and simmer for 2½ hours.

3 Add the tomatoes, tomato paste, sugar, carrots, peas, green beans, pasta, and herbs and season to taste with salt and pepper. Simmer for 20–25 minutes, until the pasta is cooked and the vegetables are tender.

4 Ladle the soup into warmed bowls and serve immediately, passing around the grated cheese separately.

Carrot & Cilantro Soup

Serves 6

ingredients
- 3 tbsp olive oil
- 1 red onion, chopped
- 1 large potato, chopped
- 1 celery stalk, chopped
- 2¾ cups chopped carrots
- 4 cups vegetable stock
- 1 tbsp butter
- 2 tsp coriander seeds, crushed
- 1½ tbsp chopped fresh cilantro, plus extra to garnish
- 1 cup milk
- salt and pepper

1 Heat the oil in a large pan. Add the onion and cook over low heat, stirring occasionally, for 5 minutes, until softened.

2 Add the potato and celery and cook, stirring occasionally, for another 5 minutes, then add the carrots and cook, stirring occasionally, for an additional 5 minutes. Cover the pan, reduce the heat to very low, and cook, shaking the pan occasionally, for 10 minutes.

3 Pour in the vegetable stock and bring to a boil, then cover and simmer for 10 minutes, until the vegetables are tender.

4 Meanwhile, melt the butter in a skillet. Add the coriander seeds and cook, stirring continuously, for 1 minute. Add the chopped cilantro and cook, stirring continuously, for 1 minute, then remove from the heat.

5 Remove the soup from the heat and let cool slightly. Transfer to a food processor or blender, in batches if necessary, and process to a puree. Return the soup to the rinsed-out pan, stir in the cilantro mixture and milk, and season to taste with salt and pepper. Reheat gently until warmed through. Ladle into warmed bowls, garnish with chopped cilantro, and serve immediately.

Roasted Vegetable Soup

Serves 6

- 2 eggplants
- 4 tomatoes
- 2 red bell peppers
- 2 onions, unpeeled
- 2 garlic cloves, unpeeled
- 4 tbsp olive oil
- fresh oregano sprig
- 7 cups chicken or vegetable stock
- salt and pepper
- chopped fresh basil, to garnish

1 Preheat the oven to 350°F/180°C. Prick the eggplants several times with a fork and put in a roasting pan. Add the tomatoes, bell peppers, unpeeled onions, and garlic. Sprinkle with 2 tablespoons of the oil. Roast in the preheated oven for 30 minutes, then remove the tomatoes. Return the other vegetables to the oven for an additional 30 minutes, until very soft and the bell pepper skins have blackened.

2 Put the cooked roasted vegetables in a bowl, cover with a damp dish towel, and let cool for 3–4 hours or overnight, until cold. When cold, cut the eggplants in half, scoop out the flesh, and put in the bowl. Remove the skin from the tomatoes, cut in half, and discard the seeds and add the flesh to the bowl. Hold the bell peppers over the bowl to collect the juices and peel off the skin. Remove the stem, core, and seeds and add the flesh to the bowl. Peel the onions, cut into quarters, and add to the bowl. Squeeze the garlic cloves out of their skins into the bowl.

3 Heat the remaining oil in a large saucepan. Add the vegetables and their juices, the leaves from the oregano sprig, and salt and pepper to taste, then cook gently for about 30 minutes, stirring frequently. Add the stock to the saucepan, bring to a boil, then simmer for 30 minutes.

4 Remove the saucepan from the heat and let cool slightly. Transfer to a food processor or blender, in batches if necessary, and process to a puree. Return the soup to the rinsed-out pan and reheat gently. Ladle into warmed bowls, garnish with basil, and serve immediately.

Curried Zucchini Soup

Serves 4

ingredients

- 2 tsp butter
- 1 large onion, finely chopped
- 3 large zucchini (about 2 lb/ 900 g), sliced
- 2 cups chicken or vegetable stock
- 1 tsp curry powder
- ½ cup sour cream, plus extra to garnish
- salt and pepper

1 Melt the butter in a large saucepan over medium heat. Add the onion and cook for about 3 minutes, until beginning to soften.

2 Add the zucchini, stock, and curry powder, along with a large pinch of salt, if using unsalted stock. Bring the soup to a boil, then reduce the heat, cover, and cook gently for about 25 minutes, until the vegetables are tender.

3 Remove the saucepan from the heat and let cool slightly. Transfer to a food processor or blender, in batches if necessary, and process to a puree. Return the soup to the rinsed-out pan, stir in the sour cream, and reheat gently but do not let it boil.

4 Taste and adjust the seasoning, if needed. Ladle into warmed bowls, garnish with a swirl of sour cream, and serve immediately.

Watercress Soup

Serves 4

ingredients

- 2 bunches of watercress (about 7 oz/200 g), thoroughly cleaned
- 3 tbsp butter
- 2 onions, chopped
- 1½ cups coarsely chopped potatoes
- 5 cups vegetable stock or water
- freshly grated nutmeg (optional)
- salt and pepper
- ½ cup yogurt or sour cream, to serve

1 Remove the leaves from the watercress and set aside. Coarsely chop the stalks.

2 Melt the butter in a large saucepan over medium heat, add the onions, and cook for 4–5 minutes, until soft. Do not brown.

3 Add the potatoes to the saucepan and mix well with the onions. Add the watercress stalks and the stock.

4 Bring to a boil, then reduce the heat, cover, and simmer for 15–20 minutes, until the potatoes are soft.

5 Add the watercress leaves and stir in gently. Remove the saucepan from the heat and let cool slightly. Transfer to a food processor or blender, in batches if necessary, and process to a puree. Return the soup to the rinsed-out pan and reheat gently. Season to taste with salt, pepper, and nutmeg, if using.

6 Ladle into warmed bowls and top each with a spoonful of yogurt and a grating of nutmeg, if using. Serve immediately.

Lettuce & Arugula Soup

Serves 4–6

ingredients

- 1 tbsp butter
- 1 large onion, halved and sliced
- 2 leeks, sliced
- 6¼ cups vegetable stock
- 6 tbsp white rice
- 2 carrots, thinly sliced
- 3 garlic cloves
- 1 bay leaf
- 2 heads of soft round lettuce (about 1 lb/450 g), cored and chopped
- ¾ cup heavy cream
- freshly grated nutmeg
- 3⅗ cups finely chopped arugula leaves, plus extra leaves to garnish
- salt and pepper
- crusty bread, to serve

1 Heat the butter in a large pan over medium heat and add the onion and leeks. Cover and cook, stirring frequently, for 3–4 minutes, until the vegetables begin to soften.

2 Add the stock, rice, carrots, garlic, and bay leaf with a large pinch of salt. Bring just to a boil. Reduce the heat, cover, and simmer for 25–30 minutes, or until the rice and vegetables are tender. Remove and discard the bay leaf.

3 Add the lettuce and cook, stirring occasionally, for 10 minutes, until the leaves are soft.

4 Remove the saucepan from the heat and let cool slightly. Transfer to a food processor or blender, in batches if necessary, and process to a puree.

5 Return the soup to the rinsed-out pan and reheat gently. Stir in the cream and a grating of nutmeg to taste. Simmer, stirring occasionally, for 5 minutes, until warmed through. Add more water or cream if you prefer a thinner soup.

6 Add the arugula and simmer, stirring occasionally, for 2–3 minutes, until it is wilted. Taste and adjust the seasoning, adding salt and pepper if needed, and ladle the soup into warmed bowls. Garnish with a few arugula leaves. Serve immediately with crusty bread.

Asparagus Soup

Serves 6

ingredients

- 1 bunch asparagus, about 12 oz/350 g
- 3 cups vegetable stock
- 4 tbsp butter or margarine
- 1 onion, chopped
- 3 tbsp all-purpose flour
- ¼ tsp ground coriander
- 1 tbsp lemon juice
- 2 cups milk
- 4–6 tbsp heavy or light cream
- salt and pepper

1 Wash and trim the asparagus, discarding the woody part of the stem. Cut the remainder into short pieces, reserving a few tips for garnish. Fine asparagus does not need to be trimmed.

2 Cook the tips in the minimum of boiling salted water for 5–10 minutes. Drain and set aside.

3 Put the asparagus stems in a saucepan with the stock, bring to a boil, cover, and simmer for about 20 minutes, until soft. Drain and reserve the stock.

4 Melt the butter in a saucepan. Add the onion and cook over low heat until soft but only barely colored. Stir in the flour and cook for 1 minute, then gradually whisk in the reserved stock and bring to a boil.

5 Simmer for 2–3 minutes, until thickened, then stir in the cooked asparagus, coriander, lemon juice, and salt and pepper to taste. Simmer for 10 minutes. Remove the saucepan from the heat and let cool slightly. Transfer to a food processor or blender, in batches if necessary, and process to a puree.

6 Return the soup to the rinsed-out pan, add the milk and reserved asparagus tips, and bring to a boil. Simmer for 2 minutes. Stir in the cream and reheat gently. Ladle into warmed bowls and serve immediately.

Spicy Vegetable Soup

Serves 4–6

ingredients

- 2 tbsp vegetable or virgin olive oil
- 1 onion, finely chopped
- 4 garlic cloves, finely chopped
- ¼–½ tsp ground cumin
- 2–3 tsp mild chili powder
- 1 carrot, sliced
- 1 waxy potato, diced
- 2 cups diced fresh tomatoes or 12 oz/350 g canned tomatoes
- 1 zucchini, diced
- ¼ small cabbage, cored and shredded
- 4 cups vegetable stock, chicken stock, or water
- 1 ear fresh corn
- 10 green or string beans, cut into bite-size pieces
- salt and pepper
- chopped fresh cilantro and sliced fresh green chile, to garnish
- tortilla chips, to serve

1 Heat the oil in a heavy-bottom pan. Add the onion and garlic and cook for a few minutes, until softened, then sprinkle in the cumin and chili powder. Stir in the carrot, potato, tomatoes, zucchini, and cabbage and cook, stirring occasionally, for 2 minutes.

2 Pour in the stock. Cover and cook over medium heat for 20 minutes, or until the vegetables are tender.

3 Meanwhile, remove and discard the husks and silks from the corn ear, then cut off the kernels using a small sharp knife. Add extra stock to the soup if needed, then stir in the corn kernels and beans and cook for an additional 5–10 minutes, or until the beans are tender. Season to taste with salt and pepper.

4 Ladle the soup into warmed bowls and garnish with cilantro and chile. Serve immediately with tortilla chips.

Garden Pea Soup

Serves 4

ingredients
- 2½ cups vegetable stock
- 3 cups shelled fresh peas
- pinch of sugar
- ½ cup light cream, plus extra to garnish
- salt and pepper
- crusty bread, to serve

1 Pour the stock into a large saucepan and bring to a boil. Add the peas and cook for 5 minutes.

2 Remove the saucepan from the heat, add the sugar, and let cool slightly. Transfer to a food processor or blender, in batches if necessary, and process to a puree.

3 Return the soup to the rinsed-out pan, stir in the cream, and reheat gently but do not let it boil.

4 Taste and adjust the seasoning, adding salt and pepper if needed. Ladle into warmed bowls and top each with a swirl of cream. Serve immediately with crusty bread.

Green Vegetable Soup

Serves 6

ingredients
- 3 tbsp olive oil
- 2 leeks, white parts only, chopped
- 2 tbsp all-purpose flour
- generous 6¾ cups vegetable stock
- 1 tsp dried thyme
- ½ tsp fennel seeds
- 1 head Boston lettuce, coarsely chopped
- 1 lb 2 oz/500 g spinach, coarse stalks removed
- 2½ cups shelled fresh or frozen peas
- 1 bunch of watercress or arugula
- ¼ cup chopped fresh mint
- salt and pepper
- 2 tbsp chopped fresh parsley, to garnish
- garlic and herb bread, to serve

1 Heat the oil in a large pan. Add the leeks and cook over low heat, stirring occasionally, for 5 minutes, until softened, then remove the pan from the heat.

2 Stir in the flour until fully incorporated, then gradually stir in the stock, a little at a time. Season to taste with salt and pepper, then add the thyme and fennel seeds.

3 Return the pan to the heat and bring to a boil, stirring continuously. Add the lettuce, spinach, peas, watercress, and mint and bring back to a boil. Boil, stirring continuously, for 3–4 minutes, then reduce the heat, cover, and simmer gently for 30 minutes.

4 Remove the soup from the heat and let cool slightly. Transfer to a food processor or blender, in batches if necessary, and process to a puree. Return the soup to the rinsed-out pan and reheat gently, stirring occasionally.

5 Ladle into warmed bowls, sprinkle with the parsley, and serve immediately with garlic and herb bread.

Soup au Pistou (French Vegetable & Pesto Soup)

Serves 4

ingredients

- 4 cups water
- 1 bouquet garni
- 2 celery stalks, chopped
- 3 baby leeks, chopped
- 4 baby carrots, chopped
- 5½ oz/150 g new potatoes, cut into bite-size chunks
- ¼ cup shelled fava beans or peas
- 6 oz/175 g canned cannellini or flageolet beans, drained and rinsed
- 3 heads of bok choy
- generous 3¼ cups arugula leaves
- pepper

pistou

- 2 large handfuls fresh basil leaves
- 1 fresh green chile, seeded
- 2 garlic cloves
- 4 tbsp olive oil
- 1 tsp freshly grated Parmesan cheese

1 Put the water and bouquet garni into a large pan and add the celery, leeks, carrots, and potatoes. Bring to a boil, then reduce the heat and let simmer for 10 minutes.

2 Stir in the fava beans and cannellini beans and let simmer for an additional 10 minutes. Stir in the bok choy, arugula, and pepper to taste and let simmer for an additional 2–3 minutes. Remove and discard the bouquet garni.

3 Meanwhile, to make the pistou, put the basil, chili, garlic, and oil into a food processor and pulse to form a thick paste. Stir in the Parmesan.

4 Stir most of the pistou into the soup, then ladle into warmed bowls. Top with the remaining pistou and serve at once.

Spinach & Ginger Soup

Serves 4

ingredients

- 2 tbsp sunflower oil
- 1 onion, chopped
- 2 garlic cloves, finely chopped
- 2 tsp chopped fresh ginger
- 8 oz/225 g baby spinach leaves
- 1 small lemongrass stalk, finely chopped
- 4 cups vegetable stock
- 1½ cups potatoes, chopped
- 1 tbsp rice wine or dry sherry
- salt and pepper
- 1 tsp sesame oil, to garnish

1 Heat the sunflower oil in a large pan. Add the onion, garlic, and ginger and cook over low heat, stirring occasionally, for 3–4 minutes, until softened.

2 Reserve eight small spinach leaves. Add the remaining leaves and lemongrass to the pan, stirring until the spinach is wilted. Add the stock and potatoes to the pan and bring to a boil. Reduce the heat, cover, and let simmer for about 10 minutes.

3 Remove the saucepan from the heat and let cool slightly. Transfer to a food processor or blender, in batches if necessary, and process to a puree.

4 Return the soup to the rinsed-out pan, stir in the rice wine, and reheat gently. Taste and adjust the seasoning, adding salt and pepper if needed.

5 Ladle into warmed bowls and top each with a drizzle of sesame oil. Garnish with the reserved spinach leaves and serve immediately.

Corn Chowder

Serves 6

ingredients

- 5½ oz/150 g unsmoked bacon, sliced into small pieces
- 2 tbsp butter
- 1 large onion, chopped
- 1 fresh bay leaf
- 5 ears fresh corn, shucked (or 4⅓ cups corn kernels)
- 2 cups milk
- 2 large garlic cloves, finely chopped
- 2 floury potatoes, cut into small chunks
- 2 cups chicken stock
- pinch of cayenne pepper
- ½ cup heavy cream
- salt and pepper
- 3 tbsp chopped fresh cilantro or flat-leaf parsley, to garnish

1 Fry the bacon in a large heavy-bottom saucepan for 5 minutes, or until starting to crisp. Add the butter, and, once foaming, the onion and bay leaf. Cover and cook over medium heat for 7–8 minutes, until the onion is soft but not colored.

2 Meanwhile, using a small sharp knife, remove the kernels from the ears of corn. Put about two-thirds of the kernels in a food processor with the milk and blend for at least 2 minutes, until smooth. Push through a fine strainer, discarding the solids left in the strainer, and reserving the liquid.

3 Add the garlic and potatoes to the pan and moisten with a little of the stock. Add the cayenne pepper and salt and pepper to taste. Cover and cook for an additional 5 minutes.

4 Pour the remaining stock and reserved corn liquid into the pan and bring to a boil. Reduce the heat and simmer, partially covered, for 5 minutes.

5 Add the remaining corn kernels and cook for an additional 5 minutes. Stir in the cream and check the seasoning, adding salt and pepper if needed. Ladle into warmed bowls, garnish with the cilantro, and serve immediately.

Gazpacho

Serves 4

ingredients

- 9 oz/250 g white bread, crusts removed
- 4¼ cups peeled and chopped tomatoes (about 1 lb 9 oz/700 g)
- 3 garlic cloves, coarsely chopped
- 2 red bell peppers, seeded and chopped
- 1 cucumber, peeled, seeded, and chopped
- 5 tbsp extra virgin olive oil
- 5 tbsp red wine vinegar
- 1 tbsp tomato paste
- 9½ cups water
- salt and pepper
- 4 ice cubes, to serve

1 Tear the bread into pieces and place in a blender. Process briefly to make breadcrumbs and transfer to a large bowl. Add the tomatoes, garlic, bell peppers, cucumber, olive oil, vinegar, and tomato paste. Mix well.

2 Working in batches, place the tomato mixture with about the same amount of the measured water in the food processor or blender and process to a puree. Transfer to another bowl. When all the tomato mixture and water have been blended together, stir well and season to taste with salt and pepper. Cover with plastic wrap and chill in the refrigerator for at least 2 hours but no longer than 12 hours.

3 When ready to serve, pour the soup into chilled bowls and float an ice cube in each bowl. Serve immediately.

Fava Bean Soup

Serves 6

ingredients

- 3¾ cups vegetable stock
- 4⅔ cups shelled fresh young fava beans
- 3 tbsp lemon juice
- 2 tbsp chopped fresh summer savory
- 6 tbsp plain yogurt, to serve
- salt and pepper
- chopped fresh mint, to garnish

1 Pour the vegetable stock into a pan and bring to a boil. Reduce the heat to a simmer, add the beans, and cook for about 7 minutes, until just tender.

2 Remove the pan from the heat and let cool slightly. Ladle into a food processor or blender, in batches if necessary, and process to a puree. Push the mixture through a strainer into a bowl.

3 Stir in the lemon juice and summer savory and season to taste with salt and pepper. Let cool completely, then cover with plastic wrap and chill in the refrigerator for at least 3 hours.

4 To serve, stir the soup, taste, and adjust the seasoning, adding salt and pepper if needed. Ladle into chilled bowls, top each with a tablespoon of yogurt, and garnish with mint. Serve immediately.

Chilled Avocado Soup

Serves 4

ingredients

- 1 tbsp lemon juice
- 2 avocados
- 1 tbsp snipped fresh chives, plus extra to garnish
- 1 tbsp chopped fresh flat-leaf parsley
- scant 2 cups cold chicken stock
- 1¼ cups light cream, plus extra to serve
- dash of Worcestershire sauce
- salt and pepper

1 Put the lemon juice into a food processor or blender. Halve the avocados and remove the pits. Scoop out the flesh and chop coarsely.

2 Place the avocado flesh, chives, parsley, stock, cream, and Worcestershire sauce in the food processor or blender and process to a smooth puree.

3 Transfer to a bowl and season to taste with salt and pepper. Cover the bowl tightly with plastic wrap and chill in the refrigerator for at least 30 minutes.

4 To serve, stir the soup and ladle into chilled bowls. Top each with a swirl of cream, garnish with chives, and serve immediately.

Chapter 2
Winter Vegetable Soups

Leek & Potato Soup

Serves 4–6

ingredients
- 4 tbsp butter
- 1 onion, chopped
- 3 leeks, sliced
- 2 potatoes, cut into
  ¾-inch/2-cm cubes
- 3½ cups vegetable stock
- salt and pepper
- ⅔ cup light cream, to serve
  (optional)
- 2 tbsp snipped fresh chives,
  to garnish

1 Melt the butter in a large saucepan over medium heat, add the onion, leeks, and potatoes, and sauté gently for 2–3 minutes, until soft but not brown. Pour in the stock, bring to a boil, then reduce the heat and simmer, covered, for 15 minutes.

2 Remove the soup from the heat and let cool slightly. Transfer to a food processor or blender, in batches if necessary, and process to a puree. Return the soup to the rinsed-out pan and reheat gently.

3 Taste and adjust the seasoning, adding salt and pepper if needed. Ladle into warmed bowls and swirl the cream on top, if using. Garnish with chives and serve immediately.

French Onion Soup

Serves 6

ingredients

- 1 tbsp olive oil
- 2 tbsp butter
- 4–5 onions, about
  1 lb 7 oz/650 g, thinly sliced
- 3 garlic cloves, finely chopped
- 1 tsp sugar
- 2 tbsp all-purpose flour
- ⅔ cup dry white vermouth
- 8¾ cups vegetable stock
- 3 tbsp brandy
- salt and pepper

cheese croûtes

- 6 slices of French bread
- 1 garlic clove, halved
- 2 cups grated Gruyère cheese

1 Heat the oil with the butter in a large pan. Add the onions and stir well, then cover, and cook over very low heat, stirring occasionally, for 15 minutes. Uncover the pan and increase the heat to medium. Stir in the the chopped garlic, sugar, and 1 teaspoon of salt, and cook, stirring frequently, for 30–40 minutes, until the onions are a deep golden brown.

2 Sprinkle the flour over the onions and cook, stirring continuously, for 3 minutes. Stir in the vermouth and cook, stirring continuously, for 2 minutes, until the alcohol has evaporated, then gradually stir in the stock and bring to a boil. Skim off any foam that rises to the surface, then reduce the heat, cover, and simmer for 40 minutes.

3 Meanwhile, make the cheese croûtes. Preheat the broiler. Toast the slices of bread on both sides. Rub each slice with the halved garlic clove, then top with the cheese and broil for a few minutes, until melted.

4 Stir the brandy into the soup, remove the pan from the heat, taste, and adjust the seasoning, adding salt and pepper if needed. Ladle into warmed bowls, top each with a cheese croûtes, and serve immediately.

Jerusalem Artichoke Soup

Serves 6

ingredients

- 1 tbsp lemon juice
- 1 lb 9 oz/700 g Jerusalem artichokes
- 4 tbsp butter
- 1 tbsp sunflower oil
- 1 large onion, chopped
- 5⅔ cups vegetable stock
- ¾ cup milk
- 1 tbsp snipped fresh chives
- scant ½ cup heavy cream
- salt and pepper
- croutons, to garnish
- extra virgin olive oil, for drizzling

1 Fill a bowl with water and stir in the lemon juice. Peel the artichokes and cut into chunks, then immediately drop them into the bowl of acidulated water to prevent discoloration.

2 Heat the butter with the sunflower oil in a large pan. Add the onion and cook over low heat, stirring occasionally, for 5 minutes, until softened. Drain the artichokes, add them to the pan, and stir well. Cover and cook, stirring occasionally, for 15 minutes.

3 Pour in the vegetable stock and milk, increase the heat to medium, and bring to a boil. Reduce the heat, re-cover the pan, and simmer for 20 minutes, until the artichokes are soft.

4 Remove the pan from the heat and let cool slightly. Add the chives and transfer the soup to a food processor or blender, in batches if necessary, and process to a puree.

5 Return the soup to the rinsed-out pan, stir in the cream, and season to taste with salt and pepper. Reheat gently, stirring occasionally, but do not let the soup boil. Ladle into warmed bowls, garnish with croutons, drizzle over the extra virgin olive oil, and serve immediately.

Parsnip Soup with
Ginger & Orange

Serves 6

ingredients
- 2 tsp olive oil
- 1 large onion, chopped
- 1 large leek, sliced
- 2 carrots, thinly sliced
- 7 parsnips (about 1 lb 12 oz/ 800 g), sliced
- 4 tbsp grated fresh ginger
- 2–3 garlic cloves, finely chopped
- grated rind of ½ orange
- 6 cups water
- 1 cup orange juice
- salt and pepper
- snipped fresh chives, to garnish

1 Heat the oil in a large saucepan over medium heat. Add the onion and leek and cook, stirring occasionally, for about 5 minutes, until softened.

2 Add the carrots, parsnips, ginger, garlic, orange rind, water, and a large pinch of salt. Reduce the heat, cover, and simmer, stirring occasionally, for about 40 minutes, until the vegetables are very soft.

3 Remove the soup from the heat and let cool slightly. Transfer to a food processor or blender, in batches if necessary, and process to a puree.

4 Return the soup to the rinsed-out pan and stir in the orange juice. Add a little water or more orange juice if you prefer a thinner consistency. Taste and adjust the seasoning, adding salt and pepper if needed. Simmer for about 10 minutes to heat through.

5 Ladle into warmed bowls, garnish with chives, and serve immediately.

Broccoli & Bleu Cheese Soup

Serves 6

ingredients

- 3 tbsp butter
- 2 white onions, chopped
- 1 large potato, chopped
- 1 lb 10 oz/750 g broccoli, cut into small florets
- 6¾ cups vegetable stock
- 5½ oz/150 g bleu cheese, diced
- pinch of ground mace
- salt and pepper
- croutons, to garnish

1 Melt the butter in a large pan. Add the onions and potato and stir well. Cover and cook over low heat for 7 minutes. Add the broccoli and stir well, then re-cover the pan and cook for an additional 5 minutes.

2 Increase the heat to medium, pour in the vegetable stock, and bring to a boil. Reduce the heat and season to taste with salt and pepper, then re-cover and simmer for 15–20 minutes, until the vegetables are tender.

3 Remove the pan from the heat, strain into a bowl, reserving the vegetables, and let cool slightly. Put the vegetables into a food processor, add a ladleful of the liquid, and process to a smooth puree. With the motor running, gradually add the remaining liquid.

4 Return the soup to the rinsed-out pan and reheat gently until very hot but not boiling. Remove from the heat and stir in the cheese until melted and thoroughly combined. Stir in the mace, taste, and adjust the seasoning, adding salt and pepper if needed.

5 Ladle into warmed bowls, sprinkle with croutons, and serve immediately.

Winter Vegetable Soup

Serves 6

ingredients

- 2 tbsp vegetable oil
- 1 large onion, thickly sliced
- 1 large potato, cut into chunks
- 3 celery stalks, thickly sliced
- 4 carrots, sliced
- 6 oz/75 g rutabaga, cut into chunks
- 4 large garlic cloves, peeled and left whole
- 6 cups chicken or vegetable stock
- 8 oz/225 g canned chopped tomatoes
- 1 leek, halved lengthwise and thickly sliced
- salt and pepper
- 2 tbsp chopped fresh flat-leaf parsley, to garnish
- grated cheddar cheese, to serve

1 Heat the oil in a large heavy-bottom saucepan over medium heat. Add the onion, potato, celery, carrots, rutabaga, and garlic cloves. Season to taste with salt and pepper, then cover and cook over medium heat, stirring occasionally, for 10 minutes.

2 Pour in the stock and tomatoes and bring to a boil. Reduce the heat and simmer, partially covered, for 30 minutes. Add the leek and cook for an additional 5 minutes, until just tender.

3 Taste and adjust the seasoning, adding salt and pepper if needed. Ladle into warmed bowls, Garnish with the parsley, sprinkle with the grated cheddar cheese, and serve immediately.

Sweet Potato & Apple Soup

Serves 6

ingredients

- 1 tbsp butter
- 3 leeks, thinly sliced
- 1 large carrot, thinly sliced
- 5 cups peeled and cubed sweet potatoes (about 1 lb 4 oz/550 g)
- 2 large tart apples, peeled and cubed
- 5 cups water
- freshly grated nutmeg
- 1 cup apple juice
- 1 cup light cream
- salt and pepper
- snipped fresh chives or chopped fresh cilantro, to garnish

1 Melt the butter in a large saucepan over low–medium heat. Add the leeks, then cover and cook, stirring frequently, for 6–8 minutes, or until soft.

2 Add the carrot, sweet potatoes, apples, and water to the saucepan and season lightly with salt, pepper, and nutmeg. Bring to a boil, then reduce the heat, cover, and simmer, stirring occasionally, for about 20 minutes, until the vegetables are very tender.

3 Remove the soup from the heat and let cool slightly. Transfer to a food processor or blender, in batches if necessary, and process to a puree.

4 Return the soup to the rinsed-out pan and stir in the apple juice. Place over low heat and simmer for about 10 minutes, until heated through.

5 Stir in the cream and continue to simmer, stirring frequently, for about 5 minutes, until heated through. Taste and adjust the seasoning, adding salt, pepper, and nutmeg if needed. Ladle the soup into warmed bowls, then garnish with chives or cilantro and serve immediately.

Cauliflower Soup

Serves 6

ingredients

- 1 tbsp olive oil
- 2 tbsp butter
- 1 large onion, coarsely chopped
- 2 leeks, sliced
- 1 large head of cauliflower
- 3¾ cups vegetable stock
- salt and pepper
- finely grated cheddar cheese and extra virgin olive oil, to serve

1 Heat the olive oil and butter in a large saucepan and cook the onion and leeks, stirring frequently, for 10 minutes, being careful not to let the vegetables color.

2 Cut the cauliflower into florets and cut the stalk into small pieces. Add to the pan and sauté with the other vegetables for 2–3 minutes.

3 Add the stock and bring to a boil, then cover and simmer over medium heat for 20 minutes.

4 Remove the soup from the heat and let cool slightly. Transfer to a food processor or blender, in batches if necessary, and process to a puree. Return the soup to the rinsed-out pan and reheat gently.

5 Taste and adjust the seasoning, adding salt and pepper if needed. Ladle into warmed bowls and top each with a spoonful of grated cheddar cheese and a drizzle of extra virgin olive oil. Serve immediately.

Creamy Mushroom &
Tarragon Soup

Serves 4–6

ingredients

- 3 tbsp butter
- 1 onion, chopped
- 1 lb 9 oz/700 g white
  mushrooms, coarsely chopped
- 3½ cups vegetable stock
- 3 tbsp chopped fresh tarragon,
  plus extra to garnish
- ⅔ cup sour cream
- salt and pepper

1 Melt half the butter in a large pan. Add the onion and cook gently for 10 minutes, until soft. Add the remaining butter and the mushrooms and cook for 5 minutes, or until the mushrooms are browned.

2 Stir in the stock and tarragon. Bring to a boil, then reduce the heat and simmer gently for 20 minutes.

3 Remove the soup from the heat and let cool slightly. Transfer to a food processor or blender, in batches if necessary, and process to a puree.

4 Return the soup to the rinsed-out pan and stir in the sour cream. Season to taste with salt and pepper. Reheat gently until warmed through. Ladle into warmed bowls and garnish with tarragon. Serve immediately.

Roasted Pumpkin, Garlic & Thyme Soup

Serves 6

ingredients
- 2 whole garlic bulbs
- 4 tbsp olive oil, plus extra for drizzling
- 2 lb/900 g pumpkin or butternut squash
- 2 tbsp fresh thyme leaves, plus extra sprigs to garnish
- 2 tbsp butter
- 1 large onion, finely chopped
- 1 tbsp all-purpose flour
- 5 cups chicken stock
- generous ⅓ cup sour cream
- salt and pepper

1 Preheat the oven to 375°F/190°C. Take two pieces of aluminum foil, each large enough to wrap a garlic bulb, and place a bulb in the center of each. Pour ½ tablespoon of the oil over each and sprinkle with salt and pepper to taste, then wrap and place in a large roasting pan. Peel and seed the pumpkin, then cut the flesh into large chunks. Toss the pumpkin in the remaining oil and sprinkle with salt and pepper to taste and half of the thyme leaves. Place in the roasting pan in a single layer and cook in the preheated oven for 1 hour.

2 Melt the butter in a large heavy-bottom saucepan. Add the onion and cook over medium heat, stirring occasionally, for 5 minutes, until soft. Stir in the flour and cook for 2 minutes. Add the stock, a few spoonfuls at a time to begin with, then add all the remainder.

3 When the pumpkin has browned, remove the roasting pan from the oven. Add the pumpkin to the pan and simmer for 10 minutes. Open the garlic packages and let cool. When cool enough to handle, break up the garlic bulbs, place the cloves on a chopping board, and press down on each until the garlic pulp squeezes out.

4 Remove the soup from the heat and let cool slightly. Stir in the garlic pulp and the remaining thyme leaves, then transfer to a food processor or blender, in batches if necessary, and process to a puree. Return the soup to the rinsed-out pan and reheat gently.

5 Ladle into warmed bowls and top each with a spoonful of the sour cream. Drizzle on a little of the oil, garnish with thyme sprigs, and serve immediately.

Celery & Bleu Cheese Soup

Serves 4

ingredients
- 2 tbsp butter
- 1 onion, finely chopped
- 4 large celery stalks, finely chopped
- 1 large carrot, finely chopped
- 4 cups chicken or vegetable stock
- 3–4 fresh thyme sprigs
- 1 bay leaf
- ½ cup heavy cream
- 5½ oz/150 g bleu cheese, crumbled
- freshly grated nutmeg
- salt and pepper
- celery leaves, to garnish

1 Melt the butter in a large saucepan over low–medium heat. Add the onion and cook, stirring frequently, for 3–4 minutes, until just softened. Add the celery and carrot and continue cooking for 3 minutes. Season lightly with salt and pepper.

2 Add the stock, thyme, and bay leaf and bring to a boil. Reduce the heat, cover, and simmer gently, stirring occasionally, for about 25 minutes, until the vegetables are very tender.

3 Remove the soup from the heat and let cool slightly. Remove and discard the thyme and bay leaf. Transfer the soup to a food processor or blender, in batches if necessary, and process to a puree.

4 Return the soup to the rinsed-out pan and stir in the cream. Simmer over low heat for 5 minutes.

5 Gradually add the bleu cheese, stirring continuously, until smooth. Do not let the soup boil. Taste and adjust the seasoning, adding salt if needed, and plenty of pepper, and nutmeg.

6 Ladle into warmed bowls, garnish with celery leaves, and serve immediately.

Potato & Pesto Soup

Serves 4

ingredients

- 2 tbsp olive oil
- 3 strips smoked bacon, chopped
- 2 tbsp butter
- 2 large starchy potatoes, finely chopped
- 2 large onions, finely chopped
- 2½ cups chicken stock
- 2½ cups milk
- 3½ oz/100 g dried conchigliette (small pasta shells)
- ⅔ cup heavy cream
- 2 tbsp chopped fresh parsley
- 2 tbsp pesto
- salt and pepper
- freshly grated Parmesan cheese, to serve

1 Heat the oil in a large saucepan and cook the bacon over medium heat for 4 minutes. Add the butter, potatoes, and onions, and cook for 12 minutes, stirring continuously.

2 Add the stock and milk to the pan, bring to a boil, and simmer for 5 minutes. Add the conchigliette and simmer for an additional 3–5 minutes.

3 Blend in the cream and simmer for 5 minutes. Add the chopped parsley, pesto, and salt and pepper to taste. Ladle the soup into warmed bowls and serve immediately with Parmesan cheese.

Chestnut & Pancetta Soup

Serves 4–6

ingredients

- 3 tbsp olive oil
- 6 oz/175 g pancetta, cut into strips
- 2 onions, finely chopped
- 2 carrots, finely chopped
- 2 celery stalks, finely chopped
- 12 oz/350 g dried chestnuts, soaked overnight and drained
- 2 garlic cloves, finely chopped
- 1 tbsp finely chopped fresh rosemary
- 4 cups chicken stock
- salt and pepper
- extra virgin olive oil, for drizzling

1 Heat the olive oil in a large pan, then add the pancetta and cook over medium heat, stirring frequently, for 2–3 minutes, or until starting to brown.

2 Add the onions, carrots, and celery and cook, stirring frequently, for 10 minutes, or until slightly golden and softened.

3 Add the chestnuts to the pan with the garlic and rosemary, then stir well.

4 Pour in the stock and bring to a simmer, then cook, uncovered, for 30–35 minutes, or until the chestnuts are beginning to soften and break down—this thickens the soup.

5 Season to taste with salt and pepper. Ladle the soup into warmed bowls, drizzle with extra virgin olive oil, and serve immediately.

Mushroom & Sherry Soup

Serves 4

ingredients

- 4 tbsp butter
- 2 garlic cloves, chopped
- 3 onions, sliced
- 1 lb/450 g mixed white and cremini mushrooms, sliced
- 3½ oz/100 g fresh porcini mushrooms, sliced
- 3 tbsp chopped fresh parsley, plus extra to garnish
- 2 cups vegetable stock
- 3 tbsp all-purpose flour
- ½ cup milk
- 2 tbsp sherry
- ½ cup sour cream
- salt and pepper

1 Melt the butter in a large pan over low heat. Add the garlic and onions and cook, stirring, for 3 minutes, until slightly softened. Add the mushrooms and cook, stirring, for an additional 5 minutes.

2 Add the parsley, pour in the stock, and season to taste with salt and pepper. Bring to a boil, then reduce the heat, cover, and simmer for 20 minutes.

3 Put the flour into a bowl, mix in enough of the milk to make a smooth paste, then stir it into the soup. Cook, stirring, for 5 minutes. Stir in the remaining milk and the sherry and cook for another 5 minutes. Remove from the heat and stir in the sour cream. Return the pan to the heat and warm gently.

4 Remove from the heat and ladle the soup into warmed bowls. Garnish with parsley and serve immediately.

Curried Vegetable Soup

Serves 4

ingredients

- 3 tbsp butter
- 2 onions, chopped
- 2 garlic cloves, finely chopped
- 1½ tsp ground cumin
- 1 tsp ground coriander
- 1 sweet potato, chopped
- 2 carrots, chopped
- 3 parsnips, chopped
- 1 tbsp curry paste
- 3 cups vegetable stock
- 3 cups milk
- 1 tsp lime juice
- 6 tbsp sour cream
- salt and pepper
- naan, to serve

fried ginger garnish

- 4-inch/10-cm piece fresh ginger
- 2 tbsp peanut oil

1 Melt the butter in a large pan. Add the onions and garlic and cook over low heat, stirring occasionally, for 8–10 minutes, until lightly browned. Stir in the cumin and coriander and cook, stirring continuously, for 2 minutes. Add the sweet potato, carrots, and parsnips and cook, stirring frequently, for 5 minutes, then stir in the curry paste and mix well. Increase the heat to medium, pour in the vegetable stock, and bring to a boil, stirring occasionally. Reduce the heat, cover, and simmer for 20–25 minutes, until the vegetables are tender.

2 Meanwhile, make the garnish. Cut the ginger into thin julienne strips. Heat the oil in a small skillet over high heat. Reduce the heat, add the ginger, and cook, stirring and twisting continuously, for 1 minute. Remove with a slotted spoon and drain on paper towels.

3 Remove the soup from the heat and let cool slightly. Transfer to a food processor or blender, in batches if necessary, and process to a puree.

4 Return the soup to the rinsed-out pan and stir in the milk. Cook, stirring occasionally, for 5 minutes. Stir in the lime juice and 3 tablespoons of the sour cream and season to taste with salt and pepper.

5 Ladle the soup into warmed bowls, add a swirl of the remaining sour cream, and garnish with the fried ginger. Serve immediately with naan.

Borscht

Serves 4

ingredients

- 5 large beets (about 2 lb 4 oz/ 1 kg)
- 5 tbsp butter
- 2 onions, thinly sliced
- 3 carrots, thinly sliced
- 3 celery stalks, thinly sliced
- 6 tomatoes, peeled, seeded, and chopped
- 1 tbsp red wine vinegar
- 1 tbsp sugar
- 2 garlic cloves, finely chopped
- 1 bouquet garni
- 5⅔ cups vegetable stock
- salt and pepper
- sour cream and rye bread, to serve
- chopped fresh dill, to garnish

1 Peel and coarsely grate 4 of the beets. Melt the butter in a large pan. Add the onions and cook over low heat, stirring occasionally, for 5 minutes, until softened. Add the grated beets, carrots, and celery and cook, stirring occasionally, for another 5 minutes.

2 Increase the heat to medium and add the tomatoes, vinegar, sugar, garlic, and bouquet garni. Season to taste with salt and pepper and stir well, then pour in the vegetable stock and bring to a boil. Reduce the heat, cover, and simmer for 1¼ hours.

3 Meanwhile, peel and grate the remaining beet. Add it and any juices to the pan and simmer for another 10 minutes. Remove the pan from the heat and let stand for 10 minutes.

4 Remove and discard the bouquet garni. Ladle the soup into warmed bowls and top each with a spoonful of sour cream. Garnish with dill and serve immediately with rye bread.

Goulash Soup

Serves 6

ingredients

- 2 tbsp olive oil
- 1 large onion, chopped
- 2 garlic cloves, finely chopped
- 3–4 carrots, thinly sliced
- ½ head of savoy cabbage, cored and shredded
- 1 small red bell pepper, seeded and chopped
- 1 tbsp all-purpose flour
- 2 tbsp sweet paprika
- 4 cups vegetable stock
- 2 potatoes, cut into chunks
- 1–2 teaspoons sugar (optional)
- salt and pepper
- sour cream, to garnish

1 Heat the oil in a large pan. Add the onion, garlic, and carrots and cook over low heat, stirring occasionally, for 8–10 minutes, until lightly colored. Add the cabbage and bell pepper and cook, stirring frequently, for 3–4 minutes.

2 Sprinkle in the flour and paprika and cook, stirring continuously, for 1 minute. Gradually stir in the vegetable stock, a little at a time. Increase the heat to medium and bring to a boil, stirring continuously. Season to taste with salt, then reduce the heat, cover, and simmer for 30 minutes.

3 Add the potatoes and bring back to a boil, then reduce the heat, re-cover the pan, and simmer for another 20–30 minutes, until the potatoes are soft but not falling apart.

4 Taste and adjust the seasoning, adding salt and pepper if needed. Stir in the sugar, if necessary. Ladle the soup into warmed bowls, swirl a little sour cream on top of each, and serve immediately.

Chapter 3
Beans & Lentils

Tuscan Bean Soup

Serves 6

ingredients

- 10½ oz/300 g canned cannellini beans, drained and rinsed
- 10½ oz/300 g canned cranberry beans, drained and rinsed
- about 2½ cups vegetable stock
- 4 oz/115 g dried conchigliette or other small pasta shapes
- 4 tbsp olive oil
- 2 garlic cloves, very finely chopped
- 3 tbsp chopped fresh flat-leaf parsley
- salt and pepper

1 Place half of the cannellini and half of the cranberry beans in a food processor or blender with half of the stock and process until smooth. Pour into a large, heavy-bottom pan and add the remaining beans. Stir in enough of the remaining stock to achieve the desired consistency, then bring to a boil.

2 Add the pasta and return to a boil, then reduce the heat and cook for 15 minutes, or until just tender.

3 Meanwhile, heat 3 tablespoons of the oil in a small skillet. Add the garlic and cook, stirring continuously, for 2–3 minutes, or until golden. Stir the garlic into the soup with the parsley.

4 Season to taste with salt and pepper and ladle into warmed soup bowls. Drizzle with the remaining olive oil and serve immediately.

Ribollita (Vegetable and Bean Soup)

Serves 6

ingredients

- 14 oz/400 g canned cannellini beans, drained and rinsed
- 3 tbsp olive oil, plus extra for drizzling
- 1 Bermuda onion, chopped
- 1 leek, chopped
- 4 garlic cloves, finely chopped
- 2 carrots, diced
- 2 celery stalks, chopped
- 2 potatoes, diced
- 2 zucchini, diced
- 2 large tomatoes, peeled, seeded, and chopped
- 1 tsp sun-dried tomato paste
- 1 dried chile, crushed (optional)
- 7½ cups vegetable stock
- 2½ cups shredded black cabbage, kale, or Swiss chard
- 2½ cups shredded savoy cabbage
- salt and pepper

croûtes

- 6 slices of ciabatta
- 2 garlic cloves, halved

1 Put half of the beans into a food processor and process briefly to a coarse puree. Scrape into a bowl and set aside.

2 Heat the oil in a large pan. Add the onion, leek, garlic, carrots, and celery and cook over low heat, stirring occasionally, for 8–10 minutes. Add the potatoes and zucchini and cook, stirring continuously, for 2 minutes.

3 Add the tomatoes, tomato paste, and dried chile, if using, and cook, stirring continuously, for 3 minutes, then stir in the bean puree. Cook, stirring continuously, for an additional 2 minutes.

4 Pour in the vegetable stock and add the black cabbage and savoy cabbage. Bring to a boil, reduce the heat, and simmer for 2 hours.

5 Toward the end of the cooking time, make the croûtes. Preheat the broiler. Rub the bread with the halved garlic cloves and toast on both sides.

6 Stir the remaining beans into the soup and heat through gently for 10 minutes. Season to taste with salt and pepper. Put a croûte in the bottom of each warmed bowl and ladle the soup over it. Drizzle with a little oil and serve immediately.

Beans & Greens Soup

Serves 4

ingredients

- 9 oz/250 g dried cannellini beans, soaked overnight and drained
- 1 tbsp olive oil
- 2 onions, finely chopped
- 4 garlic cloves, finely chopped
- 1 celery stalk, thinly sliced
- 2 carrots, halved and thinly sliced
- 5 cups water
- ¼ tsp dried thyme
- ¼ tsp dried marjoram
- 1 bay leaf
- 4½ oz/125 g leafy greens, such as Swiss chard, mustard, spinach, and kale
- salt and pepper

1 Put the beans in a saucepan and add enough cold water to cover by 2 inches/5 cm. Bring to a boil and boil for 10 minutes. Drain and rinse well.

2 Heat the oil in a large saucepan over medium heat. Add the onions, cover, and cook, stirring occasionally, for 3–4 minutes, until the onions are just softened. Add the garlic, celery, and carrots, and continue cooking for 2 minutes.

3 Add the water, drained beans, thyme, marjoram, and bay leaf. When the mixture begins to bubble, reduce the heat to low. Cover and simmer gently, stirring occasionally, for about 1¼ hours, until the beans are tender. Season with salt and pepper.

4 Let the soup cool slightly, then transfer 2 cups to a food processor or blender. Process until smooth and recombine with the soup.

5 A handful at a time, cut the greens crosswise into thin ribbons, keeping tender leaves, such as spinach, separate. Add the thicker leaves and cook gently, uncovered, for 10 minutes. Stir in any remaining greens and continue cooking for 5–10 minutes, until all the greens are tender.

6 Taste and adjust the seasoning, adding salt and pepper if needed. Ladle the soup into warmed bowls and serve immediately.

Black Bean Soup

Serves 4

- 3 tbsp corn oil
- 1 large onion, chopped
- 2 celery stalks, chopped
- 2 garlic cloves, chopped
- 2½ cups dried black beans or black-eyed peas, soaked overnight and drained
- 11¼ cups vegetable stock
- ¾ tsp cayenne pepper
- 5 tbsp lemon juice
- 2 tbsp red wine vinegar
- 2 tbsp dry sherry
- 4 hard-cooked eggs, coarsely chopped
- salt and pepper
- chopped celery leaves, to garnish
- grated cheddar cheese, to serve

1 Heat the oil in a large pan. Add the onion, celery, and garlic and cook over low heat, stirring occasionally, for 6–8 minutes, until softened.

2 Increase the heat to medium, add the beans, pour in the vegetable stock, and bring to a boil. Reduce the heat, cover, and simmer for 2–2½ hours, until the beans are tender.

3 Remove the soup from the heat and let cool slightly. Transfer all or half of the soup, depending on the texture you require, to a food processor or blender, in batches if necessary, and process to a puree.

4 Return the soup to the pan and bring just to a boil. If it is very thick, add a little water. Stir in the cayenne, lemon juice, vinegar, sherry, and hard-cooked eggs, and season to taste with salt and pepper. Reduce the heat and simmer, stirring continuously, for 10 minutes.

5 Remove the pan from the heat and ladle the soup into warmed bowls. Garnish with celery leaves, sprinkle with grated cheddar cheese, and serve immediately.

White Bean Soup
with Olive Tapenade

Serves 8

ingredients

- 12 oz/350 g dried cannellini beans, soaked overnight and drained
- 1 tbsp olive oil
- 1 large onion, finely chopped
- 1 large leek (white part only), thinly sliced
- 3 garlic cloves, finely chopped
- 2 celery stalks, finely chopped
- 2 small carrots, finely chopped
- 1 small fennel bulb, finely chopped
- 8 cups water
- ¼ tsp dried thyme
- ¼ tsp dried marjoram
- salt and pepper

tapenade

- 1 garlic clove
- 1 small bunch fresh flat-leaf parsley, stems removed
- 8½ oz/240 g almond-stuffed green olives, drained
- 5 tbsp olive oil

1 Put the beans in a saucepan and add cold water to cover by 2 inches/5 cm. Bring to a boil and boil for 10 minutes. Drain and rinse well.

2 Heat the oil in a large heavy-bottom saucepan over medium heat. Add the onion and leek, cover, and cook, stirring occasionally, for 3–4 minutes, until just softened. Add the garlic, celery, carrots, and fennel, and continue cooking for 2 minutes.

3 Add the water, drained beans, and the herbs. When the mixture begins to bubble, reduce the heat to low. Cover and simmer gently, stirring occasionally, for about 1½ hours, until the beans are very tender.

4 Meanwhile, make the tapenade. Put the garlic, parsley, and olives in a food processor or blender with the oil. Blend to a puree and scrape into a small serving bowl.

5 Remove the soup from the heat and let cool slightly. Remove and discard the thyme and bay leaf. Transfer the soup to a food processor or blender, in batches if necessary, and process to a puree.

6 Return the soup to the rinsed-out pan and thin with a little water, if necessary. Season to taste with salt and pepper, and simmer until heated through. Ladle into warmed bowls, top each with a generous teaspoon of the tapenade, and serve immediately.

Mixed Bean Soup
with Gruyère Cheese

Serves 4

ingredients

- 1 tbsp extra virgin olive oil
- 3 garlic cloves, finely chopped
- 4 scallions, sliced, plus extra
  to garnish
- 3 cups sliced mushrooms
- 4 cups vegetable bouillon
- 1 large carrot, chopped
- 14 oz/400 g canned mixed
  beans, drained and rinsed
- 1 lb 12 oz/800 g canned
  chopped tomatoes
- 1 tbsp chopped fresh thyme
- 1 tbsp chopped fresh oregano
- 1⅔ cups grated Gruyère cheese
- 4 tbsp heavy cream, plus extra
  to serve
- salt and pepper

1 Heat the oil in a large pan over medium heat. Add the garlic and scallions and cook, stirring, for 3 minutes, until slightly softened. Add the mushrooms and cook, stirring, for an additional 2 minutes.

2 Stir in the bouillon, then add the carrot, beans, tomatoes, and herbs. Season with salt and pepper. Bring to a boil, then reduce the heat and simmer for 30 minutes.

3 Remove the soup from the heat and let cool slightly. Transfer to a food processor or blender, in batches if necessary, and process to a puree.

4 Return the soup to the rinsed-out pan and stir in the cheese. Cook for an additional 10 minutes, then stir in the cream. Cook for 5 minutes, then remove from the heat. Ladle into warmed bowls and top each with a swirl of cream. Garnish with scallions and serve immediately.

Tomato & White Bean Soup

Serves 6

ingredients

- 3 tbsp olive oil
- 1⅓ cups chopped red onions
- 1 celery stalk with leaves, chopped
- 1 red bell pepper, seeded and chopped
- 2 garlic cloves, finely chopped
- 4 cups peeled and chopped plum tomatoes
- 5⅔ cups vegetable stock
- 2 tbsp tomato paste
- 1 tsp sugar
- 1 tbsp sweet paprika
- 1 tbsp butter
- 1 tbsp all-purpose flour
- 14 oz/400 g canned cannellini beans, drained and rinsed
- salt and pepper
- 3 tbsp chopped fresh flat-leaf parsley, to garnish

1 Heat the oil in a large pan. Add the onions, celery, bell pepper, and garlic and cook over low heat, stirring occasionally, for 5 minutes, until softened.

2 Increase the heat to medium, add the tomatoes, and cook, stirring occasionally, for an additional 5 minutes, then pour in the vegetable stock. Stir in the tomato paste, sugar, and sweet paprika and season to taste with salt and pepper. Bring to a boil, reduce the heat, and simmer for 15 minutes.

3 Meanwhile, mash the butter and flour to a paste in a small bowl with a fork. Stir the paste, in small pieces at a time, into the soup. Make sure each piece is fully incorporated before adding the next.

4 Add the beans, stir well, and simmer for another 5 minutes, until heated through. Ladle into warmed bowls, sprinkle with the parsley, and serve immediately.

Chunky Sweet Potato
& Lima Bean Soup

Serves 4

ingredients

- 2 tbsp olive oil
- 1 onion, chopped
- 2 celery stalks, chopped
- 1 large carrot, coarsely chopped
- 1 large or 2 small sweet potatoes, chopped
- 14 oz/400 g canned lima beans or cannellini beans, drained and rinsed
- 4 cups vegetable stock
- salt and pepper
- chopped fresh cilantro, to garnish
- freshly grated Parmesan cheese, to serve

1 Heat the oil in a large saucepan over medium heat. Add the onion, celery, and carrot and cook, stirring frequently, for 8–10 minutes, or until softened. Add the sweet potatoes and beans and cook, stirring, for 1 minute.

2 Add the stock, then stir thoroughly and bring to a simmer. Season with a little salt and pepper. Cover, then reduce the heat and cook for 25–30 minutes, or until all the vegetables are tender.

3 Remove the soup from the heat and let cool slightly, then transfer one-third of the soup to a blender or food processor and process to a puree. Return to the saucepan and mix in well. Taste and adjust the seasoning, adding salt and pepper if needed. Reheat gently until it is warmed through.

4 Ladle into warmed bowls and sprinkle the cilantro on top. Serve immediately with grated Parmesan cheese.

Red Kidney Bean
& Chorizo Soup

Serves 4

ingredients

- 2 tbsp olive oil
- 2 garlic cloves, chopped
- 2 red onions, chopped
- 1 red bell pepper, seeded and chopped
- 2 tbsp cornstarch
- 4 cups vegetable stock
- 4 potatoes, halved and sliced
- 5½ oz/150 g chorizo, sliced
- 2 zucchini, sliced
- 7 oz/200 g canned red kidney beans, drained and rinsed
- ½ cup heavy cream
- salt and pepper
- crusty bread, to serve

1 Heat the oil in a large pan. Add the garlic and onions and cook over medium heat, stirring, for 3 minutes, until slightly softened. Add the bell pepper and cook, stirring, for an additional 3 minutes.

2 In a bowl, mix the cornstarch with enough stock to make a smooth paste and stir it into the pan. Cook, stirring, for 2 minutes. Stir in the remaining stock, then add the potatoes and season to taste with salt and pepper. Bring to a boil, then reduce the heat and simmer for 25 minutes, until the vegetables are tender.

3 Add the chorizo, zucchini, and kidney beans to the pan. Cook for 10 minutes, then stir in the cream and cook for another 5 minutes. Remove from the heat and ladle into warmed bowls. Serve immediately with slices of fresh crusty bread.

Kidney Bean, Pumpkin & Tomato Soup

Serves 4–6

ingredients

- 9 oz/250 g dried kidney beans, soaked overnight and drained
- 1 tbsp olive oil
- 2 onions, finely chopped
- 4 garlic cloves, finely chopped
- 1 celery stalk, thinly sliced
- 1 carrot, halved and thinly sliced
- 5 cups water
- 2 tsp tomato paste
- ⅛ tsp dried thyme
- ⅛ tsp dried oregano
- ⅛ tsp ground cumin
- 1 bay leaf
- 14 oz/400 g canned chopped tomatoes
- 2¼ cups diced pumpkin flesh
- ¼ tsp chili paste, or to taste
- salt and pepper
- fresh cilantro, to garnish

1 Put the beans in a saucepan and add enough cold water to cover by 2 inches/5 cm. Bring to a boil and simmer for 10 minutes. Drain and rinse well.

2 Heat the oil in a large saucepan over medium heat. Add the onions, cover, and cook, stirring occasionally, for 3–4 minutes, until just softened. Add the garlic, celery, and carrot, and continue cooking for 2 minutes.

3 Add the water, drained beans, tomato paste, thyme, oregano, cumin, and bay leaf. When the mixture begins to bubble, reduce the heat to low. Cover and simmer gently, stirring occasionally, for 1 hour.

4 Stir in the tomatoes, pumpkin, and chili paste and continue simmering, stirring occasionally, for an additional 1 hour, or until the beans and pumpkin are tender. Remove and discard the bay leaf.

5 Season to taste with salt and pepper and stir in a little more chili paste, if desired. Ladle the soup into bowls, garnish with cilantro, and serve immediately.

Chickpea Soup

Serves 6

ingredients

- generous 2¼ cups dried chickpeas, soaked and drained
- 2 tbsp olive oil
- 1 onion, finely chopped
- 2 garlic cloves, finely chopped
- 1 lb/450 g Swiss chard, trimmed and finely sliced
- 2 fresh rosemary sprigs
- 14 oz/400 g canned chopped tomatoes
- salt and pepper

1 Put the chickpeas into a large pan. Add enough cold water to cover and bring to a boil, skimming off any foam that rises to the surface with a slotted spoon. Reduce the heat and simmer, adding more water if necessary, for 1–1¼ hours, until tender.

2 Drain the chickpeas, reserving the cooking water. Season the chickpeas well with salt and pepper. Put two-thirds in a food processor or blender with some of the reserved cooking water and process until smooth, adding more of the cooking water, if necessary, to produce a thinner consistency. Return to the pan.

3 Heat the oil in a medium pan, then add the onion and garlic and cook over medium heat, stirring frequently, for 3–4 minutes, or until the onion has softened. Add the Swiss chard and rosemary sprigs and cook, stirring frequently, for 3–4 minutes. Add the tomatoes and cook for an additional 5 minutes, or until the tomatoes have broken down to an almost smooth sauce. Remove and discard the rosemary sprigs.

4 Add the Swiss chard and tomato mixture to the chickpea puree and simmer for 2–3 minutes. Taste and adjust the seasoning, adding salt and pepper if needed. Ladle the soup into warmed bowls and serve immediately.

Split Pea & Ham Soup

Serves 6–8

ingredients

- 2½ cups split green peas
- 1 tbsp olive oil
- 1 large onion, finely chopped
- 1 large carrot, finely chopped
- 1 celery stalk, finely chopped
- 4 cups chicken or vegetable stock
- 4 cups water
- 8 oz/225 g lean smoked ham, finely diced
- ¼ tsp dried thyme
- ¼ tsp dried marjoram
- 1 bay leaf
- salt and pepper

1 Rinse the peas under cold running water. Put in a saucepan and add enough water to cover generously. Bring to a boil and boil for 3 minutes, skimming off the foam from the surface. Drain.

2 Heat the oil in a large saucepan over medium heat. Add the onion and cook, stirring occasionally, for 3–4 minutes, until just softened.

3 Add the carrot and celery and continue cooking for 2 minutes. Add the drained peas, pour in the stock and water, and stir to combine.

4 Bring just to a boil and stir the ham into the soup. Add the thyme, marjoram, and bay leaf. Reduce the heat, cover, and cook gently for 1–1½ hours, until the ingredients are very soft. Remove and discard the bay leaf.

5 Taste and adjust the seasoning, adding salt and pepper if needed. Ladle into warmed soup bowls and serve immediately.

Spicy Lentil & Carrot Soup

Serves 4

ingredients
- ¾ cup split red lentils
- 5 cups vegetable stock
- 3 cups carrots, sliced
- 2 onions, chopped
- 1 cup canned chopped tomatoes
- 2 garlic cloves, chopped
- 2 tbsp oil
- 1 tsp ground cumin
- 1 tsp ground coriander
- 1 fresh green chile, seeded and chopped
- ½ tsp ground turmeric
- 1 tbsp lemon juice
- 1¼ cups milk
- 2 tbsp chopped fresh cilantro
- salt
- plain yogurt, for garnish

1 Place the lentils in a large pan, together with 2½ cups of the stock, the carrots, onions, tomatoes, and garlic. Bring the mixture to a boil, then reduce the heat, cover, and simmer for 30 minutes, or until the vegetables and lentils are tender.

2 Meanwhile, heat the oil in a small pan. Add the cumin, ground coriander, chile, and turmeric and cook over low heat for 1 minute. Remove from the heat and stir in the lemon juice. Season with salt to taste.

3 Remove the soup from the heat and let cool slightly. Transfer to a food processor or blender, in batches if necessary, and process to a puree. Return the soup to the rinsed-out pan, add the spice mixture and the remaining stock, and simmer over low heat for 10 minutes.

4 Add the milk, taste, and adjust the seasoning, adding salt and pepper if needed. Stir in the fresh cilantro and reheat gently. Ladle into warmed bowls, top each with a swirl of yogurt, and serve immediately.

Bacon & Lentil Soup

Serves 4

ingredients

- 1 lb/450 g thick, rindless smoked bacon strips, diced
- 1 onion, chopped
- 2 carrots, sliced
- 2 celery stalks, chopped
- 1 turnip, chopped
- 1 large potato, chopped
- generous 2¼ cups French green lentils
- 1 bouquet garni
- 4 cups water or chicken stock
- salt and pepper

1 Heat a large, heavy-bottom pan over a medium heat. Add the bacon and cook, stirring, for 4–5 minutes, or until the fat runs. Add the onion, carrots, celery, turnip, and potato and cook, stirring frequently, for 5 minutes.

2 Add the lentils and bouquet garni and pour in the water. Bring to a boil, reduce the heat, and simmer for 1 hour, or until the lentils are tender.

3 Remove and discard the bouquet garni and season the soup to taste with pepper, and with salt if needed. Remove from the heat, ladle into warmed bowls, and serve immediately.

Squash & Lentil Soup

Serves 6

ingredients

- 3 tbsp olive oil
- 2 large onions, chopped
- 2 garlic cloves, chopped
- 2 tsp ground cumin
- 1 tsp ground cinnamon
- ½ tsp freshly grated nutmeg
- ½ tsp ground ginger
- ½ tsp ground coriander
- 2 lb 4 oz/1 kg butternut squash or pumpkin, seeded and cut into small chunks
- 1½ cups red or yellow lentils
- 7½ cups vegetable stock
- 3 tbsp lemon juice
- salt and pepper
- sour cream or plain yogurt, to garnish

1 Heat the oil in a large pan. Add the onions and garlic and cook over low heat, stirring occasionally, for 5 minutes, until softened. Add the cumin, cinnamon, nutmeg, ginger, and coriander and cook, stirring continuously, for 1 minute.

2 Stir in the butternut squash and lentils and cook, stirring continuously, for 2 minutes, then pour in the vegetable stock and bring to a boil over medium heat. Reduce the heat and simmer, stirring occasionally, for 50–60 minutes, until the vegetables are tender.

3 Remove from the heat and let cool slightly. Transfer to a food processor or blender, in batches if necessary, and process to a smooth puree.

4 Return the soup to the rinsed-out pan, and stir in the lemon juice. Taste and adjust the seasoning, adding salt and pepper if needed. Reheat gently. Ladle into warmed bowls, top each with a swirl of sour cream, and serve immediately.

Golden Vegetable Soup
with Green Lentils

Serves 6

ingredients
- 1 tbsp olive oil
- 1 onion, finely chopped
- 1 garlic clove, finely chopped
- 1 carrot, halved and thinly sliced
- 1 lb/450 g green cabbage, cored, quartered, and thinly sliced
- 14 oz/400 g canned chopped tomatoes
- ½ tsp dried thyme
- 2 bay leaves
- 6¼ cups chicken or vegetable stock
- generous 1 cup French green lentils
- 2 cups water
- salt and pepper
- chopped fresh parsley, to garnish

1 Heat the oil in a large saucepan over medium heat. Add the onion, garlic, and carrot and cook, stirring frequently, for 3–4 minutes, until the onion starts to soften. Add the cabbage and cook for an additional 2 minutes.

2 Add the tomatoes, thyme, and one of the bay leaves, then pour in the stock. Bring to a boil, reduce the heat to low, and cook gently, partially covered, for about 45 minutes, until the vegetables are tender. Remove and discard the bay leaf.

3 Meanwhile, put the lentils in a separate saucepan with the remaining bay leaf and the water. Bring just to a boil, reduce the heat, and simmer for about 25 minutes, until tender. Drain off any remaining water and set aside. Remove and discard the bay leaf.

4 When the vegetable mixture is cooked, remove from the heat and let cool slightly. Transfer to a food processor or blender, in batches if necessary, and process to a puree.

5 Return the soup to the rinsed-out saucepan and add the cooked lentils. Taste and add salt and pepper to taste, and cook for about 10 minutes to heat through. Ladle into warmed bowls, garnish with parsley, and serve immediately.

Chapter 4
Meat & Poultry

Beef & Vegetable Soup

Serves 4

ingredients

- ⅓ cup pearl barley
- 5 cups beef stock
- 1 tsp dried mixed herbs
- 8 oz/225 g lean steak, such as sirloin or tenderloin steak
- 1 large carrot, diced
- 1 leek, shredded
- 1 onion, chopped
- 2 celery stalks, sliced
- salt and pepper
- 2 tbsp chopped fresh parsley, to garnish

1 Place the pearl barley in a large saucepan. Pour in the stock and add the mixed herbs. Bring to a boil, cover, and simmer gently over low heat for 10 minutes, skimming off any foam that rises to the surface.

2 Meanwhile, trim any fat from the beef and cut the meat into thin strips.

3 Add the beef, carrot, leek, onion, and celery to the pan. Bring back to a boil, cover, and simmer for about 1 hour, or until the pearl barley, beef, and vegetables are just tender.

4 Skim away any remaining foam that has risen to the top of the soup. Blot the surface with paper towels to remove any fat. Taste and adjust the seasoning, adding salt and pepper if needed.

5 Ladle the soup into warmed bowls, garnish with parsley, and serve immediately.

Beef & Cabbage Soup

Serves 6

ingredients

- 2 tbsp vegetable oil
- 1 onion, chopped
- 2 celery stalks, diced
- 2 carrots, diced
- 1 large garlic clove, finely chopped
- ¼ tsp pepper
- 6 cups brown stock
- 1 large potato, cut into small chunks
- 2 cups cubed, cooked, corned beef, round or brisket
- 2½ cups shredded green cabbage
- salt
- 3 tbsp chopped fresh flat-leaf parsley, to garnish

1 Heat the oil in a large heavy-bottom saucepan over medium heat. Add the onion, celery, and carrots, then cover and cook, stirring occasionally, for 5–7 minutes. Add the garlic, pepper, and salt to taste, then cook for an additional minute.

2 Pour in the stock and bring to a boil. Add the potato and beef, then simmer, partially covered, for 30 minutes.

3 Add the cabbage and bring back to a boil. Reduce the heat and simmer for an additional 15 minutes, or until the cabbage is tender.

4 Taste and adjust the seasoning, adding salt and pepper if needed. Ladle into warmed bowls, garnish with the parsley, and serve immediately.

Beef Noodle Soup

Serves 6

ingredients

- ¼ cup dried Chinese mushrooms or porcini mushrooms
- 3 tbsp corn oil
- 1 lb 2 oz/500 g lean steak, such as tenderloin or sirloin, cut into thin strips
- 3 carrots, cut into julienne strips
- 10 scallions, finely shredded
- 2 garlic cloves, finely chopped
- 1 tbsp finely chopped fresh ginger
- 7½ cups vegetable stock
- 4 tbsp dark soy sauce, or to taste
- 1 tbsp hoisin sauce
- 6 tbsp Chinese rice wine or dry sherry
- 5 oz/140 g dried egg noodles
- 1⅔ cups shredded spinach leaves
- pepper

1 Put the dried mushrooms into a bowl, pour in boiling water to cover, and let soak for 20 minutes. If using Chinese mushrooms, drain and rinse. If using porcini, drain, reserving the soaking water. Strain the soaking water through a fine strainer into a bowl.

2 Heat the oil in a large pan. Add the beef and cook, stirring continuously, until browned all over. Remove with a slotted spoon and drain on paper towels.

3 Add the carrots, scallions, garlic, and ginger to the pan and cook, stirring continuously, for 5 minutes. Return the beef to the pan, pour in the vegetable stock, and add the soy sauce, hoisin sauce, and rice wine. Add the mushrooms and porcini soaking water, if using. Season to taste with pepper and bring to a boil over medium heat, then reduce the heat and simmer for 15 minutes.

4 Add the noodles and spinach to the pan, stir well, and simmer for another 7–8 minutes. Taste and adjust the seasoning, adding more pepper and soy sauce if needed. Ladle into warmed bowls and serve immediately.

Consommé

Serves 4–6

ingredients

- 5 cups strong beef stock
- 8 oz/225 g fresh extra-lean ground beef
- 2 tomatoes, skinned, seeded, and chopped
- 2 large carrots, chopped
- 1 large onion, chopped
- 2 celery stalks, chopped
- 1 turnip, chopped (optional)
- 1 bouquet garni
- 2–3 egg whites
- shells of 2–4 eggs, crushed
- 1–2 tbsp sherry (optional)
- salt and pepper
- julienne strips of raw carrot, turnip, celery, or celeriac, to garnish

1 Put the stock and ground beef in a saucepan and leave for 1 hour. Add the tomatoes, carrots, onion, celery, turnip (if using), bouquet garni, 2 of the egg whites, the crushed shells of 2 of the eggs, and plenty of salt and pepper. Bring almost to the boiling point, whisking hard all the time with a flat whisk.

2 Cover and simmer for 1 hour, being careful not to let the layer of froth on top of the soup break.

3 Pour the soup through a colander lined with two layers of clean cheesecloth into a large heatproof bowl, keeping the froth back until the end. Then pour the ingredients through the cloth again into a clean pan. The resulting liquid should be clear.

4 If the soup is not quite clear, return it to the pan with another egg white and the crushed shells of another 2 eggs. Repeat the whisking process as before and then boil for 10 minutes. Strain again.

5 Add the sherry, if using, to the soup and reheat gently. Place the garnish of vegetable strips in warmed bowls and carefully pour in the soup. Serve immediately.

Italian Meatball
& Greens Soup

Serves 4–6

ingredients

- 12 oz/350 g lean ground beef
- 4 tbsp grated onion
- 2 tbsp freshly grated Parmesan cheese, plus extra to serve
- 1 small egg, beaten
- 8 cups chicken stock
- 1½ oz/40 g dried orecchiette or other small round pasta
- 12 oz/350 g Swiss chard or savoy cabbage, stalks discarded, leaves sliced into ribbons
- salt and pepper

1 Preheat the oven to 450°F/230°C. Combine the beef, onion, Parmesan, ½ teaspoon of pepper and ½ teaspoon of salt in a bowl, mixing well with a fork. Stir in the beaten egg. Form into 24 walnut-size balls and place on a nonstick baking sheet. Cook in the preheated oven for 5–7 minutes, turning once, until lightly colored. Remove from the oven and set aside.

2 Bring the stock to a boil in a large saucepan. Add the pasta and meatballs, then simmer briskly for 10 minutes.

3 Meanwhile, steam the greens for 2–3 minutes, until wilted. Tip into a strainer and squeeze out as much liquid as possible, pressing with the back of a wooden spoon. Add the greens to the soup and cook for an additional 5 minutes, or until the greens and pasta are tender.

4 Taste and adjust the seasoning, adding salt and pepper if needed. Ladle the soup into warmed bowls and serve immediately with Parmesan cheese.

Sauerkraut & Sausage Soup

Serves 6

ingredients
- 2 tbsp butter
- 1 tbsp all-purpose flour
- 1 tbsp sweet paprika
- 8¾ cups vegetable stock
- 1 lb 7 oz/650 g sauerkraut, drained
- 1 lb 2 oz/500 g smoked pork link sausages, cut into 1-inch/2.5-cm slices
- ⅔ cup sour cream, plus extra to serve
- salt and pepper

dumplings
- ¾ cup all-purpose flour, plus extra for dusting
- pinch of salt
- 1 extra large egg

1 Melt the butter in a large pan over low heat. Add the all-purpose flour and paprika and cook, stirring continuously, for 2 minutes, then remove the pan from the heat. Gradually stir in the vegetable stock, a little at a time, until fully incorporated and the mixture is smooth.

2 Return the pan to medium heat and bring to a boil, stirring continuously. Add the sauerkraut and sausages and season to taste with salt and pepper. Reduce the heat, cover, and simmer for 30 minutes.

3 Meanwhile, make the dumplings. Sift the flour and salt into a bowl. Beat the egg in a separate bowl, then gradually beat in the dry ingredients, a little at a time. Turn out onto a floured surface and knead until smooth. Cover and let rest for 15 minutes.

4 Divide the dough into six pieces and roll into sausage shapes. Flour your hands, pinch off pieces of the dough, and add to the soup. Re-cover the pan and simmer for 5 minutes more. Remove the pan from the heat and ladle the soup into warmed bowls. Top each with a spoonful of sour cream and serve immediately.

Asian Pork Meatballs
& Greens in Broth

Serves 6

ingredients
- 8 cups chicken stock
- 3 oz/85 g shiitake mushrooms, thinly sliced
- 6 oz/175 g bok choy or other Asian greens, sliced into thin ribbons
- 6 scallions, finely sliced
- salt and pepper

pork balls
- 8 oz/225 g fresh lean ground pork
- ½ cup finely chopped spinach leaves
- 2 scallions, finely chopped
- 1 garlic clove, very finely chopped
- pinch of Chinese five-spice seasoning
- 1 tsp soy sauce

1 To make the pork balls, put the pork, spinach, scallions, and garlic in a bowl. Add the five-spice seasoning and soy sauce and mix until combined.

2 Shape the pork mixture into 24 meatballs. Place them in one layer in a steamer that will fit over the top of a saucepan.

3 Bring the stock just to a boil in a saucepan that will accommodate the steamer then adjust the heat so that the liquid bubbles gently. Add the mushrooms to the stock and place the steamer, covered, on top of the pan. Steam for 10 minutes. Remove the steamer and set aside on a plate.

4 Add the bok choy and scallions to the pan and cook gently in the stock for 3–4 minutes, or until the leaves are wilted. Taste and adjust the seasoning, adding salt and pepper if needed.

5 Divide the pork meatballs evenly among warmed bowls and ladle the soup over them. Serve immediately.

Chorizo & Kale Soup

Serves 6

ingredients

- 3 tbsp olive oil, plus extra for drizzling
- 1 Bermuda onion, finely chopped
- 2 garlic cloves, finely chopped
- 3¼ cups diced potatoes
- 6¾ cups vegetable stock
- 4½ oz/125 g chorizo or other spicy sausage, thinly sliced
- 5 cups finely shredded kale or savoy cabbage
- salt and pepper

1 Heat 2 tablespoons of the oil in a large pan. Add the onion and garlic and cook over low heat, stirring occasionally, for 5 minutes, until softened. Add the potatoes and cook, stirring continuously, for an additional 3 minutes.

2 Increase the heat to medium, pour in the vegetable stock, and bring to a boil. Reduce the heat, cover, and cook for 10 minutes.

3 Meanwhile, heat the remaining oil in a skillet. Add the chorizo and cook over low heat, turning occasionally, for a few minutes, until the fat runs. Remove with a slotted spoon and drain on paper towels.

4 Remove the pan of soup from the heat and mash the potatoes with a potato masher. Return to the heat, add the kale, and bring back to a boil. Reduce the heat and simmer for 5–6 minutes, until tender.

5 Remove the pan from the heat and mash the potatoes again to incorporate. Stir in the chorizo, season to taste with salt and pepper, and ladle into warmed bowls. Drizzle each with a little oil and serve immediately.

Hearty Winter Broth

Serves 6–8

ingredients

- 1 lb 9 oz/700 g shoulder of lamb
- 7¼ cups water
- 1 cup pearl barley, rinsed
- 2 onions, chopped
- 1 garlic clove, finely chopped
- 3 small turnips, cut into small dice
- 3 carrots, thinly sliced
- 2 celery stalks, sliced
- 2 leeks, sliced
- salt and pepper
- 2 tbsp chopped fresh parsley, to garnish

1 Cut the lamb into small pieces, removing as much fat as possible. Put into a large pan and cover with the water. Bring to a boil over medium heat and skim off any foam that rises to the surface.

2 Add the pearl barley, reduce the heat, and cook gently, covered, for 1 hour.

3 Add the prepared vegetables and season well with salt and pepper. Continue to cook for an additional hour. Remove from the heat and let cool slightly.

4 Remove the meat from the pan using a slotted spoon and strip the meat from the bones. Discard the bones and any fat or gristle. Put the meat back into the pan and let cool thoroughly, then cover and refrigerate overnight.

5 Remove the solidified fat from the surface of the soup. Reheat gently until warmed through, then season to taste with salt and pepper. Ladle into warmed bowls, garnish with parsley, and serve immediately.

North Africa Harira (Chickpea and Onion Soup)

Serves 6

ingredients

- 2 tbsp olive oil
- 8 oz/225 g boneless lean lamb, cut into cubes
- 1 onion, chopped
- ½ cup dried chickpeas, soaked overnight and drained
- 6¾ cups vegetable stock
- ½ cup red or yellow lentils
- 2 large tomatoes, peeled, seeded, and diced
- 1 red bell pepper, seeded and diced
- 1 tbsp tomato paste
- 1 tsp sugar
- 1 tsp ground cinnamon
- ½ tsp ground turmeric
- ½ tsp ground ginger
- 1 tbsp chopped fresh cilantro, plus extra to garnish
- 1 tbsp chopped fresh flat-leaf parsley
- scant ⅓ cup long-grain rice
- salt and pepper

1 Heat the oil in a large pan. Add the lamb and cook over medium heat, stirring frequently, for 8–10 minutes, until lightly browned all over. Reduce the heat, add the onion, and cook, stirring frequently, for 5 minutes, until softened.

2 Increase the heat to medium, add the chickpeas, pour in the vegetable stock, and bring to a boil. Reduce the heat, cover, and simmer for 2 hours.

3 Stir in the lentils, tomatoes, bell pepper, tomato paste, sugar, cinnamon, turmeric, ginger, cilantro, and parsley and simmer for an additional 15 minutes. Add the rice and simmer for an additional 15 minutes, until the rice is cooked and the lentils are tender.

4 Season to taste with salt and pepper and remove the pan from the heat. Ladle the soup into warmed bowls, sprinkle with cilantro, and serve immediately.

Chicken Soup

Serves 4

ingredients

- 3 tbsp butter
- 4 shallots, chopped
- 1 leek, sliced
- 1 lb/450 g skinless, boneless chicken breasts, chopped
- 2½ cups chicken stock
- 1 tbsp chopped fresh parsley
- 1 tbsp chopped fresh thyme
- ¾ cup heavy cream
- salt and pepper
- fresh thyme sprigs, to garnish
- crusty bread, to serve

1 Melt the butter in a large pan over medium heat. Add the shallots and cook, stirring, for 3 minutes, until slightly softened. Add the leek and cook for another 5 minutes, stirring. Add the chicken, stock, and herbs, and season to taste with salt and pepper.

2 Bring to a boil, then lower the heat and simmer for 25 minutes, until the chicken is tender and cooked through. Remove from the heat and let cool slightly.

3 Transfer the soup to a food processor or blender, in batches if necessary, and process to a puree. Return to the rinsed-out pan and reheat gently.

4 Stir in the cream and cook for another 2 minutes, then remove from the heat and ladle into warmed bowls. Garnish with thyme sprigs and serve immediately with crusty bread.

Chicken Soup
with Matzo Balls

Serves 4

ingredients
- 2 chicken quarters
- 11¼ cups vegetable stock
- 2 onions, chopped
- 2 celery stalks, chopped
- 2 carrots, chopped
- 2 tomatoes, peeled and chopped
- 2 fresh parsley sprigs, plus extra to garnish
- 2 oz/55 g dried vermicelli
- salt and pepper

matzo balls
- 4 tbsp butter
- ½ onion, grated
- 1 egg
- 1 egg yolk
- 1 tbsp finely chopped fresh parsley
- 1 tbsp water
- 2 cups crushed matzo crackers
- salt and pepper

1 First, make the matzo balls. Melt 1 tablespoon of the butter in a small skillet. Add the grated onion and cook over low heat, stirring occasionally, for 5 minutes, until softened. Remove from the heat and let cool.

2 Beat the remaining butter in a bowl until fluffy, then gradually beat in the egg and egg yolk. Add the parsley and the fried onion, season to taste with salt and pepper, and mix well, then beat in the water. Mix in the matzo crumbs until thoroughly incorporated. Cover and let rest in the refrigerator for 30 minutes.

3 Meanwhile, put the chicken into a large pan and pour in the vegetable stock. Bring to a boil over low–medium heat, skimming off the foam that rises to the surface. Simmer for 15 minutes.

4 Add the chopped onion, celery, carrots, tomatoes, and parsley and season to taste with salt and pepper. Reduce the heat, cover, and simmer for 50–60 minutes, until the chicken is cooked through and tender. Meanwhile, shape the matzo mixture into 18 balls.

5 Strain the soup into a clean pan, reserving the chicken quarters. Remove and discard the skin and bones and cut the meat into bite-size pieces. Add the chicken, vermicelli, and matzo balls to the pan, cover, and simmer gently for 20–30 minutes. Ladle into warmed bowls, garnish with parsley, and serve immediately.

Chicken Soup with
Ginger & Coconut Milk

Serves 4

ingredients

- 14 oz/400g skinless, boneless chicken breast portions, cut into strips
- ½ cup jasmine rice
- 1 lemongrass stalk, bruised
- 4 garlic cloves, coarsely chopped
- 2 fresh green chiles, seeded and sliced
- 4 kaffir lime leaves, torn
- 1-inch/2.5-cm piece fresh ginger, chopped
- ¼ cup chopped fresh cilantro, plus extra to garnish
- 6¾ cups vegetable stock
- 1¾ cups canned coconut milk
- 4 scallions, thinly sliced
- 1 cup baby corn
- 4 oz/115 g white mushrooms, halved
- salt
- chopped fresh red chile, to garnish

1 Put the chicken, rice, lemongrass, garlic, green chiles, lime leaves, ginger, and cilantro into a pan, pour in the vegetable stock and coconut milk, and bring to a boil over medium heat, stirring occasionally. Reduce the heat, cover, and simmer for 1 hour.

2 Remove the pan from the heat and let cool slightly. Remove and discard the lemongrass and kaffir lime leaves. Ladle the soup into a food processor or blender, in batches if necessary, and process to a puree.

3 Return the soup to the rinsed-out pan, season to taste with salt, and add the scallions, baby corn, and mushrooms. Bring back to a boil, then reduce the heat and simmer for 5 minutes.

4 Remove the pan from the heat. Ladle the soup into warmed bowls, garnish with cilantro and red chile, and serve immediately.

Chicken & Rice Soup

Serves 4

ingredients
- 6¼ cups chicken stock
- 2 small carrots, very thinly sliced
- 1 celery stalk, finely diced
- 1 baby leek, halved lengthwise and thinly sliced
- ¾ cup young green peas
- 1 cup cooked rice
- generous 1 cup sliced, cooked chicken
- 2 tsp chopped fresh tarragon
- 1 tbsp chopped fresh flat-leaf parsley, plus extra sprigs to garnish
- salt and pepper

1 Put the stock in a large saucepan and add the carrots, celery, and leek. Bring to a boil, reduce the heat to low, and simmer gently, partially covered, for 10 minutes.

2 Stir in the peas, rice, and chicken and continue cooking for an additional 10–15 minutes, or until the vegetables are tender.

3 Add the chopped tarragon and parsley, then taste and adjust the seasoning, adding salt and pepper if needed.

4 Ladle the soup into warmed bowls, garnish with parsley sprigs, and serve immediately.

Chicken Noodle Soup

Serves 6

ingredients
- 2 tbsp vegetable oil
- 1 onion, chopped
- 2 celery stalks, diced
- 3 carrots, diced
- 1 fresh thyme sprig
- 6 cups chicken stock
- 2 cups cubed skinless, boneless chicken breasts
- 1¾ oz/50 g dried egg vermicelli, broken into short pieces
- 3 tbsp chopped fresh flat-leaf parsley, to garnish
- salt and pepper

1 Heat the oil in a large, heavy-bottom saucepan over medium heat, Add the onion, celery, carrots, thyme sprig, and salt and pepper to taste. Cover and cook, stirring occasionally, for 7 minutes.

2 Pour in the stock and bring to a boil. Reduce the heat, then simmer, partially covered, for 15 minutes, until the vegetables are just tender.

3 Add the chicken and noodles. Bring back to a boil, then simmer for 10 minutes, until the chicken is cooked and the noodles are tender.

4 Taste and adjust the seasoning, adding salt and pepper if needed. Ladle into warmed bowls, sprinkle on the parsley, and serve immediately.

Curried Chicken Soup

Serves 4–6

ingredients

- 4 tbsp butter
- 2 onions, chopped
- 1 small turnip, cut into small dice
- 2 carrots, finely sliced
- 1 apple, peeled, cored, and chopped
- 2 tbsp mild curry powder
- 5 cups chicken stock
- juice of ½ lemon
- 1¼ cups small cooked chicken pieces
- 2 tbsp chopped fresh cilantro, plus extra to garnish
- salt and pepper
- ½ cup cooked rice, to serve

1 Melt the butter in a large saucepan over medium heat, add the onions, and sauté gently for 5 minutes, until soft but not brown.

2 Add the turnip, carrots, and apple and continue to cook for an additional 3–4 minutes.

3 Stir in the curry powder until the vegetables are well coated, then pour in the stock. Bring to a boil, cover, and simmer for about 45 minutes. Season well with salt and pepper and add the lemon juice.

4 Remove the soup from the heat and let cool slightly. Transfer to a food processor or blender, in batches if necessary, and process to a puree. Return the soup to the rinsed-out pan, add the chicken and cilantro, and reheat gently.

5 Place a spoonful of rice in each serving bowl and pour the soup over the top. Garnish with cilantro and serve immediately.

Turkey & Lentil Soup

Serves 4

ingredients

- 1 tbsp olive oil
- 1 garlic clove, chopped
- 1 large onion, chopped
- 3 cups sliced mushrooms
- 1 red bell pepper, seeded and chopped
- 6 tomatoes, skinned, seeded, and chopped
- generous 4 cups chicken stock
- ⅔ cup red wine
- ⅔ cup cauliflower florets
- 1 carrot, peeled and chopped
- 1 cup red lentils
- 2½ cups chopped cooked turkey
- 1 zucchini, chopped
- 1 tbsp shredded fresh basil
- salt and pepper
- crusty bread, to serve

1 Heat the oil in a large pan. Add the garlic and onion and cook over medium heat, stirring, for 3 minutes, until slightly softened. Add the mushrooms, bell pepper, and tomatoes, and cook, stirring, for an additional 5 minutes.

2 Pour in the stock and wine, then add the cauliflower, carrot, and red lentils. Season with salt and pepper. Bring to a boil, then lower the heat and simmer for 25 minutes, until the vegetables are tender and cooked through.

3 Add the turkey and zucchini to the pan and cook for 10 minutes. Stir in the basil and cook for another 5 minutes, then remove from the heat and ladle into warmed bowls. Serve immediately with crusty bread.

Turkey, Leek & Bleu
Cheese Soup

Serves 4

ingredients

- 4 tbsp butter
- 1 large onion, chopped
- 1 leek, sliced
- 2½ cups sliced cooked turkey
- 2½ cups chicken stock
- 5½ oz/150 g bleu cheese
- ⅔ cup heavy cream
- 1 tbsp chopped fresh tarragon, plus extra leaves to garnish
- pepper
- croutons, to serve

1 Melt the butter in a pan over medium heat. Add the onion and cook, stirring, for 4 minutes, until slightly softened. Add the leek and cook for an additional 3 minutes.

2 Add the turkey to the pan and pour in the stock. Bring to a boil, then reduce the heat and simmer gently, stirring occasionally, for about 15 minutes. Remove from the heat and let cool a little.

3 Transfer half of the soup to a food processor or blender and process to a puree. Return the mixture to the pan with the rest of the soup, stir in the bleu cheese, cream, and chopped tarragon and season to taste with pepper. Reheat gently, stirring.

4 Remove from the heat and ladle into warmed bowls. Garnish with chopped tarragon leaves and serve immediately with croutons.

Asian Duck Broth

Serves 4

ingredients

- 2 duck leg quarters, skinned
- 4 cups water
- 2½ cups chicken stock
- 1-inch/2.5-cm piece fresh ginger
- 1 large carrot, sliced
- 1 onion, sliced
- 1 leek, sliced
- 3 garlic cloves, crushed
- 1 tsp black peppercorns
- 2 tbsp soy sauce, or to taste
- 1 small carrot, cut into thin strips or slivers
- 1 small leek, cut into thin strips or slivers
- 3½ oz/100 g shiitake mushrooms, thinly sliced
- 1 oz/25 g watercress leaves
- salt and pepper

1 Put the duck in a large saucepan with the water. Bring just to a boil and skim off the foam that rises to the surface. Add the stock, ginger, sliced carrot, onion, leek, garlic, peppercorns, and soy sauce. Reduce the heat and simmer, partially covered, for 1½ hours.

2 Remove the duck from the stock and set aside. When the duck is cool enough to handle, remove the meat from the bones and slice thinly or shred into bite-size pieces, discarding any fat.

3 Strain the stock and press with the back of a spoon to extract all the liquid. Remove as much fat as possible. Discard the vegetables and flavoring solids.

4 Bring the stock just to a boil in a clean saucepan and add the strips of carrot and leek, the mushrooms, and duck meat. Reduce the heat and cook gently for 5 minutes, or until the carrot is just tender.

5 Stir in the watercress and continue simmering for 1–2 minutes, until it is wilted. Taste the soup and adjust the seasoning, adding a little more soy sauce if needed. Ladle the soup into warmed bowls and serve immediately.

Chapter 5
Fish & Seafood

Bouillabaisse

Serves 8

ingredients

- 2 lb 4 oz/1 kg selection of at least 4 different firm white fish fillets, such as red snapper, sea bass, eel, or monkfish, scaled and cleaned, but not skinned
- 1 lb 2 oz/500 g mussels, scrubbed and debearded
- generous ⅓ cup olive oil
- 2 onions, finely chopped
- 1 fennel bulb, finely chopped
- 4 garlic cloves, crushed
- 2 lb 6 oz/1.2 kg canned chopped plum tomatoes
- 6 cups fish stock
- pinch of saffron strands
- grated rind of 1 orange
- 1 bouquet garni
- 1 lb 2 oz/500 g cooked shrimp, shell on
- salt and pepper
- baguette, to serve

rouille

- ½ cup fresh breadcrumbs, soaked in 1 tbsp water
- 3 garlic cloves, coarsely chopped
- 1 egg yolk
- 1 fresh red chile, seeded and chopped
- ½ tsp salt
- generous ¾ cup olive oil

1 First, make the rouille. Put all of the ingredients, except the olive oil, into a food processor and blend to a paste. Keep blending and add the olive oil in a slow stream until the consistency is that of a thick mayonnaise. Chill in the refrigerator until needed.

2 Carefully pin bone the fish, then cut the fillets into bite-size pieces. Discard any mussels with broken shells and any that refuse to close when tapped. Set aside.

3 Heat the oil in a very large skillet or wide saucepan with a lid and gently fry the onion and fennel for about 15 minutes, until softened. Add the garlic and fry for 2 minutes, then add the tomatoes and simmer for 2 minutes. Stir in the stock, saffron, orange rind, and bouquet garni and bring to a boil. Simmer, uncovered, for 15 minutes.

4 Add the fish pieces, mussels, and shrimp and cover the skillet. Simmer for an additional 5–10 minutes, until the mussels have opened. Discard any that remain closed. Taste and adjust the seasoning, adding salt and pepper if needed.

5 Remove the soup from the heat and ladle into warmed bowls. Serve immediately with the rouille and baguette.

Mediterranean Fish Soup
with Aioli

Serves 4

ingredients

- 4 lb 8 oz/2 kg mixed white fish, such as sea bass, red snapper, grouper, filleted, with bones, heads, and trimmings reserved
- 2 tbsp white wine vinegar
- 2 tbsp lemon juice
- 7½ cups vegetable stock
- 2 tsp herbes de Provence
- 2 bay leaves
- 4 egg yolks
- salt and pepper
- croûtes, to serve

aioli

- salt
- 4 garlic cloves
- 2 egg yolks
- ½ cup extra virgin olive oil
- ½ cup sunflower or safflower oil
- 1–2 tbsp lemon juice

1 Cut out and discard the gills of any reserved fish heads. Cut the fish fillets into chunks. Put the fish bones, heads, and trimmings into a pan, pour in the vinegar, half of the lemon juice, and the vegetable stock, add the herbes de Provence and bay leaves, and bring to a boil. Season to taste with salt, reduce the heat, and simmer for 30 minutes.

2 Meanwhile, make the aioli. Place the garlic and salt into a mortar and pound to a paste with a pestle. Transfer to a bowl, add the egg yolks, and whisk briefly with an electric mixer until creamy. Combine the oils in a pitcher and, whisking continuously, gradually add them to the egg mixture. When about half of the oil has been incorporated, add the remainder in a thin, steady stream, whisking continuously. Stir in the lemon juice to thin to the desired consistency. Transfer the aioli to a sauce boat, cover, and set aside.

3 Strain the cooking liquid from the saucepan into a bowl and discard the contents of the strainer. Measure the cooking liquid and make up to 7½ cups with water, if necessary. Return it to the saucepan, discarding the fish heads, bones, and trimmings and the bay leaves.

4 Beat the egg yolks with the remaining lemon juice in a bowl and stir it into the pan. Add the pieces of fish, stir gently to mix, and cook over low heat for 7–8 minutes, until the fish is just cooked through and the soup has thickened. Do not let the soup boil.

5 Remove the pan from the heat and pour the soup into a warmed tureen. Serve immediately, handing around the aioli separately and accompanied by croûtes.

Italian Genovese Fish Soup

Serves 4

ingredients
- 2 tbsp butter
- 1 onion, chopped
- 1 garlic clove, finely chopped
- 2 oz/55 g rindless bacon, diced
- 2 celery stalks, chopped
- 14 oz/400 g canned chopped tomatoes
- ⅔ cup dry white wine
- 1¼ cups fish stock
- 4 fresh basil leaves, torn
- 2 tbsp chopped fresh flat-leaf parsley
- 1 lb/450 g white fish fillets (such as cod or monkfish), skinned and chopped
- 4 oz/115 g cooked peeled shrimp
- salt and pepper

1 Melt the butter in a large, heavy-bottom saucepan. Add the onion and garlic and cook over low heat, stirring occasionally, for 5 minutes, or until softened.

2 Add the bacon and celery and cook, stirring frequently, for an additional 2 minutes.

3 Add the tomatoes, wine, stock, basil, and 1 tablespoon of the parsley. Season to taste with salt and pepper. Bring to a boil, then reduce the heat and simmer for 10 minutes.

4 Add the fish and cook for 5 minutes, or until it is opaque. Add the shrimp and heat through gently for 3 minutes.

5 Ladle into warmed bowls, garnish with the remaining parsley, and serve immediately.

Fish & Sweet Potato Soup

Serves 6

ingredients

- 12 oz/350 g white fish fillet (such as cod), skinned
- scant 1 cup diced sweet potato
- 1 onion, chopped
- 2 carrots, diced
- ½ tsp ground cinnamon
- 7½ cups vegetable stock
- 14 oz/400 g clams, scrubbed
- ⅔ cup dry white wine
- 1 cup light cream
- salt and pepper
- extra virgin olive oil, for drizzling
- chopped fresh flat-leaf parsley, to garnish

1 Put the fish, sweet potato, onion, carrots, and cinnamon into a pan, pour in 4 cups of the vegetable stock, and bring to a boil. Reduce the heat, cover, and simmer for 30 minutes.

2 Meanwhile, discard any clams with broken shells and any that refuse to close when tapped. Put them into a pan, pour in the wine, cover, and cook over high heat, shaking the pan occasionally, for 3–5 minutes, until the clams have opened. Remove the pan from the heat and lift out the clams with a slotted spoon, reserving the cooking liquid. Discard any clams that remain closed. Strain the cooking liquid through a fine strainer into a bowl.

3 Remove the pan of fish and vegetables from the heat and let cool slightly. Transfer to a food processor, in batches if necessary, and process to a puree.

4 Return the soup to the rinsed-out pan, add the remaining stock and the reserved cooking liquid, and bring back to a boil. Reduce the heat and gradually stir in the cream; do not let the soup boil. Add the clams, season to taste with salt and pepper, and simmer, stirring frequently, for 2 minutes, until heated through. Garnish with parsley, drizzle with extra virgin olive oil, and serve immediately.

Miso Fish Soup

Serves 4

ingredients

- 3½ cups fish stock or vegetable stock
- 1-inch/2.5-cm piece fresh ginger, grated
- 1 tbsp mirin or dry sherry
- 1 fresh Thai chile, seeded and finely sliced
- 1 carrot, thinly sliced
- 2 oz/55 g daikon, cut into thin strips or ½ bunch radishes, sliced
- 1 yellow bell pepper, seeded and cut into thin strips
- 3 oz/85 g shiitake mushrooms, sliced if large
- 1½ oz/40 g dried fine egg noodles
- 8 oz/225 g sole fillets, skinned and cut into strips
- 1 tbsp miso paste
- 4 scallions, shredded

1 Pour the stock into a large pan and add the ginger, mirin, and chile. Bring to a boil, then reduce the heat and simmer for 5 minutes.

2 Add the carrot, daikon, yellow bell pepper, mushrooms, and noodles and simmer for an additional 3 minutes.

3 Add the fish strips with the miso paste and continue to cook for 2 minutes, or until the fish is tender. Ladle into warmed bowls, top with the scallions, and serve immediately.

Fish Soup with Broiled
Peppers & Harissa

Serves 4–6

ingredients

- 2 red or orange bell peppers
- 2–3 tbsp olive oil
- 1 onion, finely chopped
- 2–3 garlic cloves, finely chopped
- 1–2 tsp harissa
- 1 small bunch of fresh flat-leaf parsley, finely chopped
- 3½ cups fish stock
- ¾ cup fino sherry or white wine (optional)
- 14 oz/400 g canned chopped tomatoes, drained
- 2 lb 4 oz/1 kg firm-fleshed fish, such as snapper, cut into large chunks (you can add shellfish too, if you like)
- salt and pepper
- 1 small bunch of fresh cilantro, coarsely chopped, for garnishing
- crusty bread, to serve

1 Cook the bell peppers under a preheated high broiler or on a barbecue, turning frequently, for 6 to 8 minutes, or until the skin blisters and turns black. Put the charred peppers in a plastic bag and let sweat for 5 minutes, then hold by the stems under cold running water and peel off the skins. Put the bell peppers on a cutting board, remove the stems and seeds, and cut the flesh into thick strips. Set aside.

2 Heat the oil in a deep, heavy-bottom saucepan, add the onion and garlic, and cook over medium heat, stirring frequently, for 2–3 minutes, until they begin to color. Add the harissa and parsley and pour in the stock. Bring the liquid to a boil, then reduce the heat and simmer for 10 minutes to let the flavors mingle.

3 Add the sherry, if using, and the tomatoes. Gently stir in the fish and the broiled peppers and bring back to a boil. Reduce the heat, season with salt and pepper to taste, and simmer for about 5 minutes, until the fish is cooked through.

4 Ladle into warmed bowls, garnish with the cilantro, and serve immediately with crusty bread.

Cullen Skink (Scottish Fish and Potato Soup)

Serves 4–6

ingredients
- 1 lb 2 oz/500 g smoked white fish
- 1 large onion, chopped
- 4 fresh parsley sprigs, plus extra chopped parsley to garnish
- 5⅔ cups vegetable stock
- 3 large potatoes, cut into chunks
- 4 tbsp butter
- 3¾ cups milk
- salt and pepper
- crusty bread, to serve

1 Put the fish, onion, and parsley sprigs into a large pan. Pour in the vegetable stock and bring to a boil, skimming off any foam that rises to the surface. Reduce the heat, cover, and simmer for 10 minutes, until the fish flesh flakes easily.

2 Remove the pan from the heat and lift out the fish with a slotted spoon. Remove and discard the skin and bones and flake the flesh. Strain the stock and return to the rinsed-out pan.

3 Return the pan to the heat, add the potatoes, and bring back to a boil. Reduce the heat and simmer for 20–30 minutes, until tender.

4 Remove the pan from the heat. Using a slotted spoon, transfer the potatoes to a bowl, add the butter, and mash until smooth.

5 Return the pan to the heat, add the milk, and bring to a boil. Beat in the mashed potatoes, a little at a time, until thoroughly incorporated. Gently stir in the fish and season to taste with salt and pepper. Ladle into warmed bowls, garnish with chopped parsley, and serve immediately with crusty bread.

Salmon & Leek Soup

Serves 4

ingredients

- 1 tbsp olive oil
- 1 large onion, finely chopped
- 3 large leeks, including green parts, thinly sliced
- 1 potato, finely diced
- 2 cups fish stock
- 3 cups water
- 1 bay leaf
- 10½ oz/300 g skinless salmon fillet, cut into ½-inch/1-cm cubes
- ⅓ cup heavy cream
- fresh lemon juice, to taste (optional)
- salt and pepper
- fresh chervil or flat-leaf parsley sprigs, to garnish

1 Heat the oil in a heavy-bottom saucepan over medium heat. Add the onion and leeks and cook for about 3 minutes, until they begin to soften.

2 Add the potato, stock, water, and bay leaf with a large pinch of salt. Bring to a boil, then reduce the heat, cover, and cook gently for about 25 minutes, until the vegetables are tender. Remove and discard the bay leaf.

3 Remove the soup from the heat and let cool slightly. Transfer half of the soup to a food processor or blender and process to a puree. Return the mixture to the pan with the rest of the soup and stir well. Reheat gently.

4 Season the salmon with salt and pepper and add to the soup. Continue cooking, stirring occasionally, for 5 minutes, until the fish is tender and starts to break up. Stir in the cream, taste, and adjust the seasoning, adding a little lemon juice if desired. Ladle into warmed bowls, garnish with chervil, and serve immediately.

Salmon Ramen

Serves 4

ingredients

- 4 cups fish or vegetable stock
- 1 large garlic clove
- ½ tsp light soy sauce
- 4 salmon fillets, 5 oz/140 g each, skinned
- peanut or corn oil, for brushing
- 5 oz/140 g dried ramen or fine egg noodles
- 3½ cups baby spinach leaves
- 4 scallions, chopped

teriyaki glaze

- 2½ tbsp sake
- 2½ tbsp dark soy sauce
- 2 tbsp mirin or sweet sherry
- ½ tbsp brown sugar
- ½ garlic clove, very finely chopped
- ¼-inch piece fresh ginger, very finely chopped

to serve

- 1 cup fresh bean sprouts
- 1 fresh green chile, seeded and sliced
- fresh cilantro leaves

1 Preheat the broiler to high. Put the stock in a saucepan, add the garlic cloves and soy sauce, and bring to a boil for cooking the noodles.

2 Meanwhile, mix together the ingredients for the teriyaki glaze and brush one surface of each salmon fillet with the glaze. Lightly brush the broiler rack with the oil and cook the salmon under the preheated broiler for 4 minutes on one side only. The flesh should flake easily and the center should remain a bright pink. Remove the fish from the broiler and set aside.

3 Cook the noodles in the saucepan of boiling stock for 5 minutes or according to the package directions, until tender.

4 Remove the garlic from the stock, then bring the stock back to a boil. Drop in the spinach leaves and scallions and cook until the leaves are just wilted. Use a slotted spoon to remove the spinach and scallions from the pan and divide them among the warmed bowls. Divide the noodles among the bowls, then add a salmon fillet to each. Carefully pour the boiling stock into each bowl.

5 Sprinkle with the bean sprouts, chile slices, and cilantro leaves and serve immediately.

Hot & Sour Shrimp Soup

Serves 2

ingredients

- 10½ oz/300 g large shrimp, peeled and deveined
- 2 tsp vegetable oil
- 2 fresh red chiles, sliced
- 1 garlic clove, sliced
- about 3 cups fish stock
- 4 thin slices fresh ginger
- 2 lemongrass stalks, bruised
- 5 kaffir lime leaves, shredded
- 2 tsp jaggery or light brown sugar
- 1 tbsp chili oil
- handful of fresh cilantro leaves
- dash of lime juice

1 Dry-fry the shrimp in a skillet or wok until they turn pink. Remove and set aside.

2 Heat the vegetable oil in the same skillet, add the chiles and garlic, and cook for 30 seconds.

3 Add the stock, ginger, lemongrass, lime leaves, and sugar and simmer for 4 minutes. Add the reserved shrimp with the chili oil and cilantro and cook for 1–2 minutes.

4 Stir in the lime juice, ladle into warmed bowls, and serve immediately.

Laksa (Shrimp and Vegetable Soup)

Serves 4

ingredients

- 1 tbsp corn oil
- 2–3 garlic cloves, cut into thin slivers
- 1–2 fresh red chiles, seeded and sliced
- 2 lemongrass stalks, outer leaves removed, chopped
- 1-inch/2.5-cm piece fresh ginger, grated
- 5 cups fish or vegetable stock
- 12 oz/350 g large shrimp, shelled and deveined
- 4 oz/115 g shiitake mushrooms, sliced
- 1 large carrot, grated
- 2 oz/55 g dried egg noodles (optional)
- 1–2 tsp Thai fish sauce
- 1 tbsp chopped fresh cilantro, plus extra sprigs to garnish

1 Heat the oil in a large pan over medium heat, add the garlic, chiles, lemongrass, and ginger and cook, stirring frequently, for 5 minutes. Add the stock and bring to a boil, then reduce the heat and let simmer for 5 minutes.

2 Stir in the shrimp, mushrooms, and carrot. If using the egg noodles, break into small pieces, add to the pan, and let simmer for an additional 5 minutes, or until the shrimp have turned pink and the noodles are tender.

3 Stir in the Thai fish sauce and cilantro and heat through for an additional minute. Ladle into warmed bowls, garnish with cilantro sprigs, and serve immediately.

Quick Scallop Soup
with Pasta

Serves 6

ingredients

- 1 lb 2 oz/500 g prepared scallops
- 1½ cups milk
- generous 6¾ cups vegetable stock
- generous 1 cup frozen baby peas
- 6 oz/175 g dried taglialini
- 5 tbsp butter
- 2 scallions, finely chopped
- ¾ cup dry white wine
- 3 slices of prosciutto, cut into thin strips
- salt and pepper
- chopped fresh flat-leaf parsley, to garnish

1 Slice the scallops in half horizontally and season to taste with salt and pepper.

2 Pour the milk and vegetable stock into a pan, add a pinch of salt, and bring to a boil. Add the peas and pasta, bring back to a boil, and cook for 8–10 minutes, until the pasta is tender but still firm to the bite.

3 Meanwhile, melt the butter in a skillet. Add the scallions and cook over low heat, stirring occasionally, for 3 minutes. Add the scallops and cook for 45 seconds on each side. Pour in the wine, add the prosciutto, and cook for an additional 2–3 minutes.

4 Stir the scallop mixture into the soup, taste, and adjust the seasoning, if needed. Ladle into warmed bowls, garnish with parsley, and serve immediately.

Manhattan Clam Chowder

Serves 6

ingredients
- 1 tsp sunflower oil
- 4 oz/115 g salt pork or unsmoked bacon, diced
- 1 onion, finely chopped
- 2 celery stalks, chopped
- 4 tomatoes, peeled, seeded, and chopped
- 3 potatoes, diced
- pinch of dried thyme
- 3 tbsp chopped fresh parsley
- ⅔ cup tomato juice
- 2½ cups vegetable stock
- 36 quahog or littleneck clams, scrubbed
- ⅔ cup dry white wine
- salt and pepper
- crusty bread, to serve

1 Heat the oil in a pan. Add the salt pork and cook over medium heat, stirring frequently, for 6–8 minutes, until golden brown. Remove with a slotted spoon.

2 Add the onion and celery to the pan, reduce the heat to low, and cook, stirring occasionally, for 5 minutes, until softened. Increase the heat to medium and add the tomatoes, potatoes, thyme, and parsley.

3 Return the pork to the pan, season to taste with salt and pepper, and pour in the tomato juice and vegetable stock. Bring to a boil, stirring continuously, then reduce the heat, cover, and simmer for 15–20 minutes, until the potatoes are just tender.

4 Meanwhile, discard any clams with broken shells and any that refuse to close when tapped. Put them into a separate pan, pour in the wine, cover, and cook over high heat, shaking the pan occasionally, for 4–5 minutes, until the shells have opened.

5 Remove the clams with a slotted spoon and let cool slightly. Discard any clams that remain closed and remove the remainder from their shells. Strain the cooking liquid through a cheesecloth-lined strainer into the soup.

6 Add the clams to the soup and heat through, stirring continuously, for 2–3 minutes. Remove from the heat, taste, and adjust the seasoning, adding salt and pepper if needed. Ladle into warmed bowls and serve immediately with crusty bread.

New England
Clam Chowder

Serves 4

ingredients
- 2 lb/900 g clams, scrubbed
- 4 bacon strips, chopped
- 2 tbsp butter
- 1 onion, chopped
- 1 tbsp chopped fresh thyme
- 1 large potato, diced
- 1¼ cups milk
- 1 bay leaf
- 1⅔ cups heavy cream
- 1 tbsp chopped fresh parsley
- salt and pepper

1 Discard any clams with broken shells and any that refuse to close when tapped. Put the remainder into a large pan with a splash of water. Cook over high heat for 3–4 minutes, until they open. Discard any that remain closed. Strain, reserving the cooking liquid. Set aside until cool enough to handle, reserving some for a garnish.

2 Remove the clams from their shells, chopping them roughly if large, and set aside.

3 In a clean pan, dry-fry the bacon until browned and crisp. Drain on paper towels and reserve. Add the butter to the same pan and, when it has melted, add the onion. Cook for 4–5 minutes, until soft but not colored. Add the thyme and cook briefly before adding the potato, reserved cooking liquid, milk, and bay leaf. Bring to a boil and simmer for 10 minutes, or until the potato is just tender.

4 Remove the soup from the heat and let cool slightly. Remove and discard the bay leaf, then transfer the soup to a food processor or blender, in batches if necessary, and process to a puree.

5 Return the soup to the rinsed-out pan and add the clams, bacon, and cream. Simmer for another 2–3 minutes, until heated through. Season to taste with salt and pepper. Stir in the parsley and ladle into warmed bowls. Garnish with the reserved clams in their shells and serve immediately.

Mussel Soup

Serves 6

ingredients

- 48 mussels, scrubbed and debearded
- 1 onion, finely chopped
- 2 tbsp chopped fresh flat-leaf parsley
- 2 bay leaves
- generous 1 cup hard cider
- 4 tbsp butter
- 2 celery stalks, chopped
- 2 leeks, thinly sliced
- 2½ cups milk
- ⅓ cup all-purpose flour
- 2½ cups vegetable stock
- pinch of freshly grated nutmeg
- ½ tsp fennel seeds
- 1 cup heavy cream
- salt and pepper
- whole wheat bread, to serve

1 Discard any mussels with broken shells and any that refuse to close when tapped. Sprinkle the onion, parsley, and bay leaves over the bottom of a large saucepan and put the mussels on top. Season to taste with salt and pepper and pour in the hard cider. Cover, bring to a boil over high heat, and cook, shaking the pan occasionally, for 4–5 minutes, until the mussels have opened.

2 Remove the pan from the heat and lift out the mussels. Discard any that remain closed. Remove the remainder from their shells and set aside. Strain the cooking liquid into a bowl.

3 Melt the butter in a separate large pan. Add the celery and leeks and cook over low heat, stirring occasionally, for 8 minutes, until lightly browned. Meanwhile, pour the milk into another pan and bring just to a boil, then remove from the heat.

4 Sprinkle the flour over the vegetables and cook, stirring continuously, for 2 minutes. Increase the heat to medium and gradually stir in the milk, a little at a time, then stir in the vegetable stock. Bring to a boil, stirring continuously, then reduce the heat, and simmer for 15 minutes.

5 Remove the pan from the heat and strain the soup into a bowl. Return to the rinsed-out pan, add the reserved cooking liquid, the nutmeg, fennel seeds, and mussels, and season to taste with salt and pepper. Return to the heat and stir in the cream. Reheat gently for a few minutes but do not let the soup boil. Ladle into warmed bowls and serve immediately with whole wheat bread.

Carrot & Mussel Soup

Serves 4–6

ingredients

- 2 lb 4 oz/1 kg carrots
- 7 tbsp butter
- 1 tsp sugar
- 5⅔ cups vegetable stock
- 48 mussels, scrubbed and debearded
- 1¼ cups dry white wine
- 1 garlic clove, coarsely chopped
- salt and pepper
- 2 tbsp chopped fresh flat-leaf parsley, to garnish
- whole wheat bread rolls, to serve

1 Reserve 3 of the carrots and slice the remainder. Melt 4 tablespoons of the butter in a large pan. Add the sliced carrots and half of the sugar and cook over low heat, stirring occasionally, for 5 minutes. Increase the heat to medium, pour in the vegetable stock, season to taste with salt, and bring to a boil. Reduce the heat, cover, and simmer, stirring occasionally, for about 25 minutes.

2 Meanwhile, finely chop the reserved carrots. Melt the remaining butter in a small pan. Add the chopped carrots and the remaining sugar and cook over low heat, stirring occasionally, for 10 minutes. Remove from the heat.

3 Discard any mussels with broken shells and any that refuse to close when tapped. Put the remainder into a pan, pour in the wine, and add the garlic. Cover and cook over high heat, shaking the pan occasionally, for 4–5 minutes, until the mussels have opened. Remove the pan from the heat and lift out the mussels. Discard any that remain closed. Remove the mussels from their shells. Strain the cooking liquid through a cheesecloth-lined strainer into a bowl.

4 Remove the pan of carrots from the heat and let cool slightly. Transfer to a food processor, add the mussels cooking liquid, and process to a puree. Return the soup to the rinsed-out pan, season to taste with salt and pepper, and reheat. Gently stir the mussels into the soup along with the carrot-and-sugar mixture. Ladle into warmed bowls, garnish with parsley, and serve immediately with bread rolls.

Cajun Crab & Corn
Chowder

Serves 6

ingredients
- 3 tbsp butter
- 1 onion, finely chopped
- 2 garlic cloves, finely chopped
- 2 celery stalks, finely chopped
- 1 small carrot, finely chopped
- ¾ cup medium-dry white wine
- 2¼ cups vegetable stock
- 1½ cups frozen corn kernels
- pinch of cayenne pepper
- ½ tsp dried mixed herbs
- 1½ cups heavy cream
- ¾ cup sour cream
- 1 tbsp chopped fresh dill
- 8 oz/225 g white crabmeat
- salt and pepper
- whole wheat bread rolls, to serve

1 Melt the butter in a large pan. Add the onion, garlic, celery, and carrot and cook over low heat, stirring occasionally, for 5 minutes, until softened.

2 Increase the heat to medium, pour in the wine, and cook for 2 minutes, until the alcohol has evaporated. Pour in the vegetable stock and bring to a boil, then add the corn, cayenne, and mixed herbs. Bring back to a boil, reduce the heat, and simmer for 15 minutes.

3 Add the heavy cream and simmer gently over very low heat for an additional 10–15 minutes; do not let the soup boil.

4 Gradually add the sour cream, whisking continuously with a balloon whisk, then stir in the dill and crabmeat and season to taste with salt and pepper. Heat gently for 3–4 minutes, then ladle into warmed bowls and serve immediately with bread rolls.

Lobster Bisque

Serves 4

ingredients

- 1 lb/450 g cooked lobster
- 3 tbsp butter
- 1 small carrot, grated
- 1 celery stalk, finely chopped
- 1 leek, finely chopped
- 1 small onion, finely chopped
- 2 shallots, finely chopped
- 3 tbsp brandy
- ¼ cup dry white wine
- 5 cups water
- 1 tbsp tomato paste
- ½ cup heavy cream, or to taste
- 6 tbsp all-purpose flour
- 2–3 tbsp water
- salt and pepper
- snipped fresh chives, to garnish

1 Pull off the lobster tail. With the legs up, cut the body in half lengthwise. Scoop out the tomalley (the soft, pale greenish-gray part) and, if it is a female, the roe (the solid red-orange part). Reserve these together, covered and refrigerated. Remove the meat and cut into bite-sized pieces, then cover and chill in the refrigerator. Chop the shell into large pieces.

2 Melt half of the butter in a large saucepan over medium heat and add the lobster shell pieces. Cook until brown sediment begins to stick to the bottom of the pan. Add the carrot, celery, leek, onion, and shallots. Cook, stirring, for 1½–2 minutes (do not let it burn). Add the brandy and wine and bubble for 1 minute. Pour in the water, add the tomato paste and a large pinch of salt, and bring to a boil. Reduce the heat and simmer for 30 minutes, then strain the stock, discarding the solids.

3 Melt the remaining butter in a small saucepan and add the tomalley and roe, if any. Add the cream and whisk to mix well, then remove from the heat and set aside.

4 Put the flour in a small mixing bowl and very slowly whisk in the cold water. Stir in a little of the hot stock mixture to make a smooth liquid.

5 Bring the remaining lobster stock to a boil and whisk in the flour mixture. Boil gently for 4–5 minutes, or until the soup thickens. Press the tomalley-and-cream mixture through a strainer into the soup, then add the lobster meat. Simmer until heated through.

6 Taste the soup and adjust the seasoning, adding salt and pepper if needed. Stir in a little more cream if you like. Ladle into warmed bowls, garnish with chives, and serve immediately.

Chapter 6
Accompaniments

Croutons

Serves 4–6

ingredients

- 2 slices day-old white, whole wheat, or whole grain bread, crusts removed
- 4 tbsp vegetable or olive oil
- 1 garlic clove, finely chopped (optional)
- finely chopped fresh herbs, such as parsley and thyme (optional)
- ½ tsp paprika or chili powder (optional)
- 1 tbsp freshly grated Parmesan cheese (optional)
- salt and pepper

1 Cut the bread into ½-inch/1-cm cubes.

2 Heat the oil in a skillet, add the garlic, if using, and cook for 1 minute. Add the bread cubes in a single layer, tossing occasionally until they are golden brown and crisp.

3 Remove the pan from the heat and spoon out the croutons onto paper towels to drain.

4 While the croutons are still hot, toss them in the fresh herbs, paprika, or Parmesan, if using. Season to taste with salt and pepper. The croutons are best used on the day of making.

Seeded Bread Rolls

Makes 8

ingredients

- 3⅓ cups white bread flour, plus extra for dusting
- 1 tsp salt
- 1½ tsp active dry yeast
- 1 tbsp vegetable oil, plus extra for brushing
- 1½ cups lukewarm water
- 1 egg, beaten
- sesame or poppy seeds, for sprinkling

1 Place the flour, salt, and yeast in a large bowl and mix well. Pour in the oil and add the water, then mix well to make a smooth dough.

2 Turn out onto a lightly floured surface and knead well for 5–7 minutes, until smooth and elastic. Brush a bowl with oil. Shape the dough into a ball, place it in the bowl, and cover with a damp dish towel. Let rise in a warm place for 1 hour, until the dough has doubled in volume.

3 Turn out the dough onto a lightly floured surface and knead briefly until smooth. Divide the dough into eight pieces. Shape the dough into round rolls. Place the rolls on a baking sheet.

4 Cover the rolls with a damp dish towel and let rise for 30 minutes, until the rolls have doubled in size.

5 Preheat the oven to 425°F/220°C. Brush the rolls with the beaten egg and sprinkle with seeds. Bake in the preheated oven for 10–15 minutes, until golden brown. Test that the rolls are baked by tapping on the bottoms with your knuckles—they should sound hollow. Transfer to a wire rack to cool.

Crusty White Bread

Makes 1 loaf

ingredients

- 1 egg
- 1 egg yolk
- ¾–1 cup lukewarm water
- 4½ cups white bread flour, plus extra for dusting
- 1½ tsp salt
- 2 tsp superfine sugar
- 1 tsp active dry yeast
- 2 tbsp butter, diced
- vegetable oil, for brushing

1 Lightly beat together the egg and egg yolk in a measuring cup. Stir in enough lukewarm water to make up to 1¼ cups.

2 Sift the flour and salt together into a bowl and stir in the sugar and yeast. Add the butter and rub it in with your fingertips until the mixture resembles breadcrumbs. Make a well in the center, pour in the egg mixture, and stir well with a wooden spoon until the dough begins to come together, then knead with your hands until it leaves the side of the bowl. Turn out onto a lightly floured surface and knead well for about 10 minutes, until smooth and elastic.

3 Brush a bowl with oil. Shape the dough into a ball, put it into the bowl, and cover with a damp dish towel. Let rise in a warm place for 1–2 hours, until the dough has doubled in volume.

4 Brush a 7½ x 4½ x 3½-inch/ 19 x 12 x 9-cm loaf pan with oil. Turn out the dough onto a lightly floured surface, punch down with your fist, and knead for 1 minute. With lightly floured hands, shape the dough into a rectangle the same length as the pan and flatten slightly. Fold it lengthwise into 3 and place in the prepared pan, seam-side down. Cover with a damp dish towel and let rise in a warm place for 30 minutes, until the dough has reached the top of the pan.

5 Preheat the oven to 425°F/220°C. Bake the loaf for 30 minutes, until it has shrunk from the sides of the pan, is golden brown, and sounds hollow when tapped on the bottom with your knuckles. Transfer to a wire rack to cool.

Whole Wheat Harvest
Bread

Makes 1 loaf

ingredients

- 2 cups whole wheat bread flour, plus extra for dusting
- 1 tsp salt
- 1 tbsp nonfat dry milk
- 2 tbsp soft brown sugar
- 1 tsp active dry yeast
- 1½ tbsp vegetable oil, plus extra for brushing
- ¾ cup lukewarm water

1 Sift the flour and salt together into a bowl, tip in the bran from the sifter, and stir in the milk, sugar, and yeast. Make a well in the center and pour in the oil and lukewarm water. Stir well with a wooden spoon until the dough begins to come together, then knead with your hands until it leaves the side of the bowl. Turn out onto a lightly floured surface and knead well for about 10 minutes, until smooth and elastic.

2 Brush a bowl with oil. Shape the dough into a ball, put it into the bowl, and cover with a damp dish towel. Let rise in a warm place for 1 hour, until the dough has doubled in volume.

3 Brush a 6½ x 4¼ x 3¼-inch/ 17 x 11 x 8-cm loaf pan with oil. Turn out the dough onto a lightly floured surface, punch down with your fist, and knead for 1 minute. With lightly floured hands, shape the dough into a rectangle the same length as the pan and flatten slightly. Fold it lengthwise into 3 and place in the prepared pan, seam-side down. Cover with a damp dish towel and let rise in a warm place for 30 minutes, until the dough has reached the top of the pan.

4 Preheat the oven to 425°F/220°C. Bake the loaf for about 30 minutes, until it has shrunk from the sides of the pan, the crust is golden brown, and it sounds hollow when tapped on the bottom with your knuckles. Transfer to a wire rack to cool.

Mixed Seed Bread

Makes 1 loaf

ingredients

- 3¼ cups white bread flour, plus extra for dusting
- scant 1¼ cups rye flour
- 1½ tsp salt
- 1½ tbsp nonfat dry milk
- 1 tbsp light brown sugar
- 1 tsp active dry yeast
- 1½ tbsp sunflower oil, plus extra for brushing
- 2 tsp lemon juice
- 1¼ cups lukewarm water
- 1 tsp caraway seeds
- ½ tsp poppy seeds
- ½ tsp sesame seeds

topping

- 1 egg white
- 1 tbsp water
- 1 tbsp sunflower or pumpkin seeds

1 Sift both types of flour and the salt together into a bowl and stir in the milk, sugar, and yeast. Make a well in the center and pour in the oil, lemon juice, and lukewarm water. Add the seeds. Stir well with a wooden spoon until the dough begins to come together, then knead with your hands until it leaves the side of the bowl. Turn out onto a lightly floured surface and knead well for about 10 minutes, until smooth and elastic.

2 Brush a bowl with oil. Shape the dough into a ball, put it into the bowl, and cover with a damp dish towel. Let rise in a warm place for 1 hour, until the dough has doubled in volume.

3 Brush a 9 x 5 x 3-inch/23 x 13 x 8-cm loaf pan with oil. Turn out the dough onto a lightly floured surface, punch down with your fist, and knead for 1 minute. With lightly floured hands, shape the dough into a rectangle the same length as the pan and flatten slightly. Fold it lengthwise into three and place in the pan, seam-side down. Cover with a damp dish towel and let rise in a warm place for 30 minutes, until the dough has reached the top of the pan.

4 Preheat the oven to 425°F/220°C. For the topping, lightly beat the egg white with the water in a bowl. Brush the top of the loaf with the egg white glaze and sprinkle with the seeds. Bake in the preheated oven for 30 minutes, until golden brown and the loaf sounds hollow when tapped on the bottom with your knuckles. Transfer to a wire rack to cool.

Rye Bread

Makes 1 loaf

ingredients
- 5 cups rye flour
- scant 1⅔ cups white bread flour, plus extra for dusting
- 2 tsp salt
- 2 tsp light brown sugar
- 1½ tsp active dry yeast
- scant 2 cups lukewarm water
- 2 tsp vegetable oil, plus extra for greasing

glaze
- 1 egg white
- 1 tbsp cold water

1 Sift the flours and salt together into a bowl. Add the sugar and yeast and stir to mix. Make a well in the center and pour in the water and oil. Stir until the dough begins to come together, then knead until it leaves the side of the bowl. Turn out onto a lightly floured surface and knead for 10 minutes, until elastic and smooth.

2 Brush a bowl with oil. Shape the dough into a ball, put it in the bowl, cover, and let rise in a warm place for 2 hours, or until doubled in volume.

3 Oil a baking sheet. Turn out the dough onto a lightly floured surface and punch down, then knead for 10 minutes. Shape the dough into a ball, put it on the prepared baking sheet, and cover. Let rise in a warm place for another 40 minutes, or until doubled in volume.

4 Meanwhile, preheat the oven to 375°F/190°C. Beat the egg white with the water in a bowl. Bake the loaf in the preheated oven for 20 minutes, then remove from the oven and brush the top with the egg white glaze. Return to the oven and bake for another 20 minutes.

5 Brush the top of the loaf with the glaze again and return to the oven for another 20–30 minutes, until the crust is a rich brown color. Transfer to a wire rack to cool.

Irish Soda Bread

Makes 1 loaf

ingredients

- 2 cups white all-purpose flour, plus extra for dusting
- 2 cups whole wheat flour
- 1½ tsp baking soda
- 1 tsp salt
- 1 tsp brown sugar
- 1¾ cups buttermilk

1 Preheat the oven to 450°F/230°C. Dust a baking sheet with flour. Sift the flours, baking soda, and salt into a bowl and stir in the sugar. Make a well in the center and pour in enough of the buttermilk to make a dough that is soft but not too wet and sticky. Add a little more buttermilk, if necessary.

2 Turn the dough out onto a floured surface and knead very briefly into a large circle, about 2 inches/5 cm thick. Dust lightly with flour and, using a sharp knife, mark the top of the loaf with a deep cross.

3 Place the loaf on the prepared baking sheet and bake in the preheated oven for 15 minutes. Reduce the oven temperature to 400°F/200°C and bake for an additional 20–25 minutes, or until firm and golden brown. Test that the loaf is baked by tapping on the bottom with your knuckles—it should sound hollow. Transfer to a wire rack to cool.

Buttermilk Biscuits

Serves 4

Makes 6–7

ingredients
- 1⅔ cups all-purpose flour
- 1 tsp salt
- 1 tsp baking soda
- 1 tsp cream of tartar
- ¼ tsp pepper
- 4 tbsp unsalted butter
- ⅔ cup buttermilk or sour cream
- beaten egg yolk, to glaze

1 Sift the flour, salt, baking soda, and cream of tartar into a bowl. Sift again to mix thoroughly. Stir in the pepper.

2 Rub in the butter using your fingertips until the mixture resembles fine breadcrumbs. Make a well in the center and pour in the buttermilk. Mix with a fork to form a soft dough. Turn out onto a floured surface and knead very lightly until the dough is smooth.

3 Roll out the dough to a thickness of ¾ inch/2 cm. Stamp out circles using a 2½-inch/6-cm round cutter. Let stand for 15 minutes.

4 Preheat the oven to 425°F/220°C. Put a nonstick baking sheet in the oven to heat. Brush the biscuits with the beaten egg yolk and place on the sheet. Bake in the preheated oven for 15 minutes, until brown and well risen. Transfer to a wire rack to cool.

Chile Cornbread Muffins

Makes 12

ingredients
- 1¼ cups all-purpose flour
- 4 tsp baking powder
- 1¼ cups cornmeal
- 2 tbsp superfine sugar
- 1 tsp salt
- 4 scallions, finely chopped
- 1 fresh red chile, seeded and finely chopped
- 3 eggs, beaten
- ⅔ cup plain yogurt
- ⅔ cup milk

1 Preheat the oven to 400°F/200°C. Put 12 paper muffin liners in a 12-hole muffin pan.

2 Sift the flour and baking powder into a large bowl. Stir in the cornmeal, sugar, salt, scallions, and chile.

3 Beat together the eggs, yogurt, and milk, then pour into the flour mixture and beat until just combined. Spoon the mixture into the muffin liners.

4 Bake the muffins in the preheated oven for 15–20 minutes, until risen, golden, and just firm to the touch. Transfer to a wire rack to cool.